Published by New Forge Books

First printing: August 2016

Printed by **Reprowest**
A CIP catalogue for this title is available from the British Library.
ISBN: **978-1-900114-05-9**

DEDICATION

Dedicated to my wife Bernie, sons Bryan and Damian and grandchildren, Jane and Ben. This is also for Josephine DeCourcey, her brother, Marty, and sister, Brid who, with the late Eoin King, have been great Connemara friends for many years.

ACKNOWLEDGEMENT

This book could not have been produced without the generous assistance of John Sweeney, of the Station House Hotel, Clifden. The Station House is one of Connemara's best appointed, friendliest and most welcoming places to stay.

Illustrations include photographs of Seamus Heaney, Richard Murphy, Patrick Kavanagh, Louis MacNeice, John McGahern, Paul Durcan, Ethel Mannin, Peter O'Toole, Robert Shaw, Mary Ure, Moya Cannon, Jennifer Johnston, Sheddy Feeney, Eoin King and Tomas Coohill plus a host of Connemara seascapes, landscapes, interesting people and places by Bill Heaney, Heather Greer, Peter Walsh and Rodger Scullion.

Chapter 1

THE BACK OF BEYOND

Wild Atlantic Way, the road from Clifden to Leenane and Westport by Bill Heaney

'It was a country I had always known, mournful and gay inhabitants, moonstone air and bloody with fuchsias. The mountains had never woken up and the sea had never gone to sleep ...' **– Louis MacNeice on Connemara.**

It has often been called ***The Back of the Back of Beyond***. Connemara is lovely, lonely, wild and windswept. But whether its endless golden beaches, boulder-strewn fields, chocolate brown peat bogs and soaring, blue mountains are under siege from sheets of Atlantic rain, sunk in rolling sea mist or swaddled in warm summer sunshine, Connemara is constantly enthralling. Connemara's beauty is as magnificent as its mountains, lakes and fjords and as permanent as the streams and swift-flowing salmon rivers that skip, surge and tumble ever downwards in their rush to the sea. All year round there is a riot of colour in the hills and hedgerows. Bright yellow flowers burst forth on dark green gorse bushes; blood red fuchsia abounds. Bronze montbretia sway and dance in the breeze; foxgloves and yellow flag irises, white clover and bell heather intermingle on the riverbanks.

The interminable Atlantic blanket bog stretches out over rain-washed fields in ubiquitous waterlogged hollows. Sections of the bog, which have been used over centuries for cutting turf to keep Connemara's home fires burning, are now home to sphagnum moss, bog cotton, myrtle, butterwort and heath spotted orchids. Trees have a hard struggle for survival here. The older ones are estimated to have been standing for only 80-100 years. There are sycamore and ash plantings and some Monterey pines but the distribution of oak is patchy and many other species display evidence of damage from the storms that blow the salt-laden, hedge-scorching wind in off the ocean. However, when the sun shines in Connemara you will feel that you have died and woke up in Heaven. There is nowhere in the world like this magical land of *Iar Connacht,* a veritable showcase for Mother Nature to display all her considerable wares and weather, and both of them often on the same day.

Having just arrived via the A59, the Wild Atlantic Way, I negotiate the wide expanse of Clifden's recently rain-peppered main street and duck into the paper shop next door to the Post Office. Clifden is the capital of Connemara. I want to catch up on the news and my request is for two national newspapers, the *Irish Times* and the *Irish Independent,* and the *Connacht Tribune,* the long-established local newspaper. The *Tribune* is packed with news and hatches, matches and dispatches. The memorial notices carry photographs of the deceased, many of them long departed but never forgotten. In Connemara people are precious. There is traditionally a great hunger here for news. And what is contained in the intimations columns of the newspapers is essential information for those newly-landed into town. For many of the residents who no longer go to church on Sunday to hear the family notices read out by the priest or the rector, it is important to know who has just recently come into the world and who has gone from it. Knowledge of what is happening where, and to whom, helps greatly when it comes to joining in conversation in Connemara, although most of that nowadays centres mainly on politics and farming and fishing – and money, of course. That particular topic has been on local lips since the collapse of the banks and now Brexit. Austerity hasn't gone away you know. My own greeting in the newsagent's shop, naturally, includes a reference to the weather outside in the street.
The wind has been blowing hard of late and the tail end of yet another hurricane is forecast. Everything that can be tied down has been tied down under big red and blue tarpaulins, which add splashes of colour to the green and brown fields and gardens. The tarpaulins are secured with iron stakes, washed up fishing nets, old ropes and strategically placed boulders. My pessimistic outlook on the weather is met by a sanguine response from the woman behind as busy a shop counter as ever you'll come across. The board between us is piled high with papers, packets of sweets, picture postcards, souvenirs, knick knacks and the usual holiday town paraphernalia. The shop lady sums up the widely-held Connemara folk's philosophy --- 'Ah, now, lookit, aren't we the lucky ones? We could be living, Lord help us, in one of those places where they have had a tsunami, or maybe even an earthquake, or both. Or even a horrible terrorist war. The wind and the rain can be a scourge at times, but at least we survive it.' Anyway, who cares about the skin-soaking rain, the scorching wind and the occasional Force 12 that strikes this place suddenly with Atlantic fury? It's all hugely spectacular for the visitor, and in Connemara there are so many warm and snug places to shelter; to hide away from the worst of that loud weather, and so many interesting people to meet, especially during the Clifden Arts Festival.
You can mingle while standing over a creamy-headed pint of black stout in a pub or seated in the corner of a cosy Clifden café sipping Cappuccino Connemara or a heart-warmingly hot Irish coffee. Connemara folk, open and friendly, will greet you with a smile and 'how are ye?' Or, if you have been here before 'You're welcome back. It's nice to see you again'. Clifden, with its houses and shops painted a myriad of bright colours and with its remarkable modern 'cheese grater' sculpture and stylish street furniture in the Market Square, celebrated the 200th anniversary of its founding in 2012. It has the name of being a Johnny come lately, having arrived on the Irish tourist scene only recently. This is misleading. Clifden may have started out as a stark 19th century prison town, but visitors who have come here for many years – and keep coming back - for necessary rest, relaxation, swimming and sport have found a *cead mile failte* (a hundred thousand welcomes) on everyone's lips and on every doorstep.

Clockwise: Clifden Bookshop in Main Street; Way to go – sign for the golf course and Ballyconneely; Market Square en fete and Moran's Medical Hall.

It was around 1940 that the novelist Sean O'Faolain, in his widely-acclaimed book *An Irish Journey* urged visitors to the West of Ireland to get out and about and meet the people. He wrote: 'Do not for Connemara's sake take up residence in the famous tourist hotels. (The proprietors need not, if they read this, be chafed: the people for whom I write are the few and discriminating, usually the poor, not the 'Grand Hotel' people who buy guide-books full of asterisks and descriptions of antiquities.) Lift the latch in any promising house and share the hearth with the people. Share the smells and the fleas, if necessary. The *vin du pays* is strong. Having come this far you would be a fool not to get drunk on it. The price is that lifted latch, for nowhere is there such warm, hearty and hospitable folk as here. Every cottage has its welcome. The roads belong to every man. The mountain paths lead to conversations on the way. Take every boreen. Clamber over every tumbling wall. Rejoice if out of these frayed crannies all of a sudden your eyes are blasted by the beauty of the phantasms of the rainbows that come and go in the sun-shot aqueous air.'

The artist Paul Henry, who accompanied O'Faolain on his journey, captured the quality of the light in the blue and brown and gold landscapes. His paintings of huge lakes, tiny fields, tumbling walls and peat bogs are masterpieces. Henry's paintings now hang in the homes of the rich and famous and in art galleries across Europe and America. One of these paintings, found in an English attic and brought for valuation to BBC television's Antiques Road Show, was estimated to be worth a fortune. It is 80 years since Paul Henry so skilfully painted these landscapes and seascapes and Sean O'Faolain described them so vividly that you could almost

smell the perfume of the turf smoke as you journeyed through that book. The fleas have long since taken their leave of Connemara's ancient cottages with their, thatched roofs, half doors, earthen floors, wooden settles, hair mattresses and hens scampering under the kitchen table. The thatch has been replaced in many instances by emigrants to America, Canada, Scotland and England who 'sent home the slates'.
Many of today's homes of Connemara are modern bungalows with all mod cons. And Sean O'Faolain's 'grand hotels' are no longer exclusive to the rich and famous. They have been complemented by new hotel complexes, such as the Station House Hotel in Clifden, which has comfortable beds and modern facilities, including its own theatre, cinema, swimming pool, shops, railway and Connemara pony museums and other attractions to suit every taste. Ordinary people can afford to stay in these hotels. Modest budgets can be accommodated.
Prosperity, like world peace, came dropping slowly in Connemara, but drop it eventually did, and the accommodation in farmhouses and guest houses for the residents, as for the visitors, is first class. The visitor scene has changed, changed utterly, and the discriminating persons who stay here will find that the bedrooms are warm and comfortable and that the full Irish breakfasts are superb. Fish, prime beef, Connemara lamb, which have grazed on herbs on the slopes of the towering Twelve Pins, and vegetables grown in kitchen gardens, are on offer in the restaurants. The chefs seek to appeal to every appetite and meet every taste. There is freshly caught lobster, scallops in their shells, crabs claws and crayfish and mussels and oysters by the dozen. A wide variety of fish including plaice, brill, turbot, sole, pollack and mackerel are landed from local boats. The food and wine are top drawer. MasterChef fans eat your heart out. In these 21st century guest houses, restaurants and hotels, there are sturdy walls and pleasant décor, dining rooms without draughts, bathrooms en suite with steaming hot showers, central heating and comfortable sitting rooms complete with wifi, television sets and turf fires. There are, in addition, panoramic views from picture windows of the Connemara shoreline rising steeply to the constantly changing mountains, the highest of which is 3,000 feet.

Padraig Post ready to deliver to homes across the Connemara countryside. And a busker plays outside in the Market Square. *Pictures by Bill Heaney.*

The vast Connemara canopy of intensely blue sky and milky white clouds is breath-taking. And often, after the showers of 'a soft day,' there are rainbows, magnificent rainbows. There are in addition tiny harbours where brightly-painted blue and red ferries are tied up to bollards on stone piers waiting to take fresh victuals, provisions and visitors to the offshore islands. These lie long, low and shark-shaped five miles out from the Cleggan shore. Visitors in walking gear mingle with islanders in the queue on the quay. These are the very same islands James Joyce referred to in his epic novel, *Ulysses*. Joyce scholars will draw your attention to the moment when Leopold Bloom passes by St Joseph's National School on his dalliance from Dalkey through the streets of Dublin. He sees through a classroom window a teacher taking a class of boys at their 'joggerfry' lessons. They are being told about Inishturk, Inishark and Inishbofin and the people who live there. Currachs, black as the tar used in their delicate skin and wooden frame construction, dance on their moorings near fishing boats and luxury yachts in the harbours. Larger work boats are tied up at the pier or moored and protected by the bluff quay walls. If you're lucky you'll catch sight of a traditional, red-sailed Galway hooker, so keep your camera close-by you at all times. I once witnessed from a high stool in Oliver's pub, cattle being brought ashore from one of these hookers by farmers and fishermen using a block and tackle on the quay. That memorable sight has stuck with me for years.

On Inishbofin and out by Cleggan and Claddaghduff you will hear the call of the cuckoo and the corncrake in the meadows along the shore. And around by Aughrus Point, Sellerna and Rosadillisk keep your eyes peeled for seals. You might even see a dolphin. There are safe, sandy beaches here to go swimming. Take one of the short circular country walks from the village and you may come across men harvesting turf on the bog. Or become a rider to sea and take a horse from the Cleggan Riding Centre across the mountain to Claddaghduff and the over the vast strand and causeway to Omey Island. All roads lead to Clifden and the verges and hedges are a riot of red fuchsia, which are also called *lachrima Christi*, the tears of Christ. The Sky Road is awesome.

Whether you drive, cycle – and cycling is greatly encouraged here - or take Shanks's Pony you cannot fail to be impressed by the spectacular views of the Atlantic and the windy flock of offshore islands. You can see the Slyne Head lighthouse and the White Lady, a navigational aid which stands erect and on guard on the shore. It is an exhilarating walk out from Clifden past the Hughes' family's popular Abbeyglen Hotel, the D'Arcy Monument, Clifden Castle and the old coastguard station, which has been converted to holiday apartments. The tarred road takes you out to Streamstown Bridge and on to the main road into town again.

Connemara's fields are a riot of colour and even on a wet evening the views from the Sky Road are spectacular. *Pictures by Bill Heaney*

Friendly donkey and Connemara ponies on a soft day at Claddaghduff.

Look out for wild flowers pushing their way through the slate-like thin yellow stone walls by the roadside. These are the famine walls which were built by poor labourers at the time of the Great Hunger, the notorious Famine of the 19th century. The miniscule fields, bounded by dry stone walls, are stocked with sturdy, rust-coloured cattle; Scottish black-faced sheep; silver Connemara ponies, and the occasional, friendly donkey. Brightly plumed red, black and white hens, ducks, geese and turkeys range freely in the gardens of some houses.

Set aside a whole day for a visit to the Connemara National Park on Diamond Mountain in Letterfrack or stately Kylemore Abbey, the school founded by nuns from Belgium. Or the surgeon/author Oliver St John Gogarty's country house at Renvyle, which is now a welcoming family and fisherman's hotel. In Connemara the *mna teach* – the women of the house – especially out by Claddaghduff and Cleggan, and on the island of Inishbofin, and their husbands and partners, some of whom still fish the sea and farm the land, will welcome you into their homes and look after you as though you are one of the family. They'll feed you up on soda bread and good Irish butter and sausages and bacon and fresh eggs and coffee and steaming hot tea. Some of them will make you a memorable dinner.

The hotels will welcome you, too, of course, but the experience is not quite the same, or so personal, as when you press the bell on a farmer or fisherman's door and share the fireside with a family in any promising house. How could it be? Connemara is not the back of the back of beyond at all, of course. What Connemara is beyond is our wildest dreams when it comes to wonderful holidays and warm hospitality; it is one of *the* places in the world to visit. You will be made most welcome here. Clifden, Cleggan, Claddaghduff and Inishbofin are places you will come to with a sense of escape and part from with great reluctance. If, as that old Bing Crosby song goes, a little bit of heaven really did fall out the sky one day, then that precious morsel must be this corner of Connemara. This last outcrop of Europe, clinging precariously to the edge of the world, really is a place where the mountains have never woken up and the sea has never gone to sleep. It is somewhere to cherish and recall and remember for the rest of your days.

People waiting on the pier at Cleggan to board the Island Discovery, the ferry for Inishbofin. Pat Concannon and his crew welcome All Ireland Free Travel Scheme and Northern Ireland Smart Pass Holders. Inishbofin Island is a very popular venue for weddings because of its unique atmosphere, magnificent facilities and breath-taking scenery. They even lay on special ferry transportation arrangements for guests. School tours are also very popular as are artist and photography short breaks. For special group rates, give them a call on +353 95 45819 or M: 086 1718829 / 087 3667185 or e mail: info@inishbofinislanddiscovery.com *Pictures by Bill Heaney*

Chapter 2
POETS' PARADISE

Famous Seamus Heaney, who visited Clifden, Cleggan and Inishbofin.
Picture by John Minihan

Cleggan poet Richard Murphy tells a great story about meeting Patrick Kavanagh in McDaid's public house off fashionable Grafton Street in the city of Dublin. Turned out by the landlord with fellow topers on to the street at 2.30pm – there was no drinking allowed in Dublin in the afternoon to comply with the licensing laws at the time – Murphy asks Kavanagh where he can get a copy of his book *The Great Hunger*, which is out of print. Kavanagh replies that it just so happens that he is going that very afternoon to meet up with the wife of W. B. Yeats and, if Murphy gives him the loan of ten shillings, he will obtain one from her and pass it on to him later. 'Later' turns out to be five years down the road at a poetry reading in the ballroom of Dublin's Royal Hibernian Hotel, where Kavanagh, notoriously irascible, shy and short of money, stands outside the door listening to the proceedings rather than pay up to get in. Richard Murphy never did get his ten bob back. Patrick Kavanagh was not, unfortunately so far as I know, one of the many, glitterati and literati and stars of stage and screen whom Richard Murphy brought to the tiny Connemara fishing village of Cleggan and the nearby island of Inishbofin. Patrick did visit the Connemara Gaeltacht, however, when he went walkabout in the West of Ireland. Had Kavanagh been there leaning on the mahogany in either Eileen O'Malley's Pier Bar in Cleggan, awaiting the island ferry, or entertaining the fishermen in Miko Day's Inishbofin public house, the farmer poet from Monaghan would doubtless have made his presence felt.

Poets who did make the journey out to Cleggan, and from there to the Island of the White Cow – and, more importantly, made it back again - included the Nobel laureate Seamus Heaney; the

Pulitzer Prize winning American poet Theodore Roathke; the English poet laureate Ted Hughes and his iconic, exceptionally beautiful and ultimately tragic wife, Sylvia Plath. Roathke, who became a great favourite with the fishermen, got carried away with the warmth of the hospitality and overdid the imbibing of bottles of red wine, pints of stout and tumblers of golden whiskey in the dark, smokey confines of Miko's. Unfortunately, Theodore, who was affectionately known as Ted, was eventually whisked away to dry out in East Galway in the county mental hospital at Ballinasloe. It was agreed he was not well when he decided to make his bed under the stars on the pier at Inishbofin. His successful recovery was happily assisted along the way by the fact that the resident psychiatrist in Ballinasloe conveniently turned a blind eye to his taking time out intermittently to carouse with and booze with the consultants and nursing staff.

Seamus Heaney with his portrait by Colin Davidson and the cover of Heaney's *New Selected Poems 1966-1987* published by Faber and Faber.

Rothke's fellow poet Seamus Heaney was not just a 'notable', but a Nobel laureate, and this is a few lines of the poem *Seeing Things* in which he recalled a trip he made to the island of Inishbofin in Connemara:

Sunlight, turf smoke, seagulls, boatslip, diesel.
One by one we were being handed down
Into a boat that dipped and shilly-shallied
Scaresomely every time. We sat tight …

Published by Faber and Faber

The Swinging Sixties may well have been psychedelic elsewhere in the world, but the village of Cleggan was largely depressed with little employment and many of its young people having to emigrate to find work. Even its wonderful scenery had failed to cheer the people up. Cleggan and the surrounding area had undergone a whole series of tragedies and setbacks. In its heyday at the beginning of the 20th century, according to the historian Tim Robinson, there were about eighteen sailing craft and forty-eight currachs working out of Cleggan Bay. The fishery employed nearly 500 people. Fish from Cleggan could be at the Billingsgate Market in London the morning after it was landed. There had been accidents involving considerable loss of life both in Cleggan and Inishbofin in the first half of the century and the port lost most of its herring and mackerel fishing fleet following the closure of the Clifden-Galway railway line, which was used to export their catch. The village was sombre and subdued with just a few old shops cum public houses in it before the poet Richard Murphy arrived on the scene.

Clifden railway station which is now part of a superb hotel and leisure complex called the Station House Hotel.

Murphy was high born. His parents were Sir William Murphy, the British ambassador to the Bahamas, and his debutante wife, Betty Ormsby. The couple were married at Luss Parish Church near her family home on Loch Lomondside in Scotland. Their son was desperate to make his name as a poet and craved peace and tranquillity in a place where he would be inspired to sit down and write. To that end he purchased and refurbished an old Galway hooker in Inishbofin to set up a tourism business to fund his poetry project. Murphy persuaded Inishbofin islander Pat Concannon, a survivor of the Cleggan Disaster and eponymous forebear of the present island ferryman, to teach him to sail the old boat. And then he introduced sailing and fishing holidays to the area, giving it much needed shot in the arm. The Cleggan folk and Inishbofin islanders, who had plenty of spirit and resilience, began to thrive on his encouragement. He was such a successful businessman that he soon had two Galway hookers operating out of Cleggan and was able to give work to local fishermen and families working in hotels and earning income from taking paying guests into their homes. He also made enough money to have an impressive pink granite house designed for himself by a Scottish architect and built by local craftsmen. Soon he had his long dreamed of bolthole by the harbour.

Cleggan suddenly had a spring in its step. A Breton company had set up a lobster fishery back at Aughrusmore and fishermen concentrated on laying lobster pots in Cleggan Bay which was kept free from fish farms to keep pollution out. Visitor numbers increased and many of them took the mail boat to Inishbofin, where they walked and went fishing and bird watching and relaxed by the shore. The Cleggan pubs took on a new lease of life. The once dark, nicotine-stained décor was jettisoned and they began to serve seafood and coffee and teas. People came to enjoy swimming on the secluded beaches and to walk over the drumlins and down to Sellerna. The name of this hamlet comes from the Gaelic word *sailearnach*, a place where willow rods are grown for use in making lobster pots. W B Yeats made such places famous and romantic in his poem *Down by the Salley Gardens:*

Down by the salley gardens my love and I did meet;
She passed the salley gardens with little snow-white feet.

Posh, polished and articulate, this former public schoolboy is a grandson of Canon Richard Murphy, once rector of the Church of Ireland's Christ Church, which hosts one of the two landmark spires in Clifden. A graduate of Oxford University, he craved success as a writer. Over six foot tall and 'built like a fishing rod', Murphy had presence and was a strikingly handsome young man. He dressed in a hand knitted oatmeal Aran gansey, a navy blue nautical cap with a gold anchor on the skip and hand-woven, grey Connemara tweed trousers. These were often sunk into rubber Wellington boots. Over these traditional clothes he wore when it rained – and it rains often in Connemara - a stylish black, belted, calf-length oilskin coat. That was how Richard Murphy was attired when I was first introduced to him by Eoin King of Aughrusbeg in Ulick and Bunny Joyce's public house in Cleggan.
Eoin was one of a number of craftsmen from the village, carpenters and stone masons, who were employed by 'Mr Murphy' to build him that house at the pier head. It was with stones from the collapsed walls of the old cabins, like Eoin King's grandparents' place at Aughrusbeg, which were eventually demolished or had just fallen down, that Richard Murphy built *The New Forge*, the house to which he brought his wife, the poet, writer, doctor and heiress, Patricia Avis, and their daughter, Emily. The wife's wealth and Murphy's Oxbridge and diplomatic service connections attracted, in addition to poets, eminent writers such as John McGahern, whose many books include *That They May Face The Rising Sun* and *Amongst Women.* McGahern's first book, *The Dark,* was banned in the 1950s by the Irish Government censors and cost him his job as a teacher in a Leitrim school managed by the parish priest for the Irish Catholic Church. Of course, that incident also made McGahern famous. There is nothing like being a banned author to boost book sales.
Encouragement for new writers is contained in a quote from him: 'I think technique can be taught but I think the only way to learn to write is to read, and I see writing and reading as completely related. One almost couldn't exist without the other.' There may be a nod to Connemara in this quote from the great man: 'Ireland is a peculiar society in the sense that it was a nineteenth century society up to about 1970 and then it almost bypassed the twentieth century.' And in the fact that fishing plays a significant role in McGahern's depiction of rural life, its pastimes and economies. *Nightlines* (1970) is one of the most distinguished of his short-story collections.

Robert Shaw and his Scottish sweetheart, actress Mary Ure.
Pictures by Moviephotostills

Movie stars too came to Cleggan, including megastars of the Hollywood firmament such as Peter O'Toole and his actress wife, Sian Phillips. O'Toole, who was the star of producer David Lean's 1959 blockbuster movie, *Lawrence of Arabia*, and *Jaws* star Robert Shaw and his lovely Scottish wife, Mary Ure, also stayed with Richard Murphy in Cleggan. Mary, who suffered deep depression and died at the age of just 43, was brought up in Helensburgh at Cairndhu on the Firth of Clyde and learned to sail with yachting friends on the Gareloch, off Kilcreggan. The indomitable and imperious Katharine Hepburn and the notorious hell raiser Sir Anthony Hopkins also found their way to Clifden during the 1968 filming by the shores of Lough Corrib of *Lion in Winter.* A budding young actress, Brenda Fricker, who was to make her name and star in both films and, most memorably, the long-running BBC Saturday night television series *Casualty* was a regular visitor with her sister, Grainne, a promising young writer, on holidays from Dublin. They stayed with their Conroy relations at the old coastguard station high on a hill looking out towards Cleggan Head. Steve McQueen, who made the *Mackintosh Man* at Roundstone, Sharon Stone, Sting, Mary Black, Frances Tumelty, John Hurt, John Nettles and James Bolam and his wife, Susan Jameson, are others in a cast of hundreds who were seduced by Connemara's charms and came to Clifden, Cleggan and Claddaghduff to rest and relax. And let their hair down when the mood took them. I recall a hilarious exchange in Oliver's pub which involved one of these handsome film stars and a young, local woman. He was chatting her up at the bar when a red-haired man warned him: 'Leave that woman alone. That's her husband sitting over there in the corner – and I'm her lover.'

I met the notorious hell-raiser Peter O'Toole in E J King's popular public house on the corner of Main Street and Market Street in Clifden. I am sure this was before this famous pub was bought by the Sweeney family from Claddaghduff. Eoin King always insisted that we should, if ever spending money anywhere, support our neighbours and friends. And Joseph and Maisie Sweeney and their children, all of whom later became successful in business, were good friends. Peter O'Toole, who was sitting on a high stool at the bar in E J King's holding court in the company of a few worthies, some hangers on and some minders, picked up on my Scottish accent when I ordered a pint of Guinness. He beckoned me over to join him and asked where I came from. My Scottish burr was very like his mother's, he said. She was a Scottish nurse who gave birth to him either in Connemara or Yorkshire. He claimed the great event happened in Clifden and said he had a birth certificate to prove it. However, inconveniently for Peter O'Toole – because he has always been desperate to be actually Irish rather than nominally so – there was still extant somewhere another birth certificate which said he was born in Leeds. From what I can recall of our conversation, which isn't a great deal since the Guinness and red wine – red ink, he called it – was flying and our meeting took place a long time ago, he said his mother came from Stirlingshire. He nodded sagely to those around him when I said that I had been born in Stirlingshire, in the town of Bridge of Allan, at Airthrey Castle no less, in 1945. 'I knew your accent was just like my mother's,' he said. He was impressed when I mentioned the castle and even more so when I added that it is now part of the campus of Stirling University. It had been turned into a maternity hospital during the Second World War when all the expectant mothers from Clydeside were been shipped out to the countryside to have their babies in relative safety following the devastation wrought by the Luftwaffe in the Clydebank Blitz of March 1941. The only problem with Peter O'Toole's theory about his mother and I having a similar accent, which I diplomatically didn't mention, was that I had spent only a few days in Stirlingshire as an infant immediately after my birth and had been brought up 40 miles away in Dumbarton, where the accent is quite different. The Scottish accent I acquired on Clydeside is much broader and more working class, more Glasgow if you like, than Stirling. Anyway, all journalists are classless and I knew that O'Toole had, like me, worked for a living as a junior reporter on his local newspaper at Pudsey in Yorkshire. He had then gone off to join the Royal Navy. At least half of this I knew to be true – the part about him having worked on a newspaper. I was aware of it because one of my journalist colleagues, the man who had employed me and encouraged me in newspapers, the late Gerry Fitzgerald, had spoken about working for the same local paper as Peter O'Toole. We talked about that and about Gerry who also loved the sea and ships to the extent that he was nicknamed Para Handy, the skipper of the Clyde puffer *Vital Spark* in Neil Munro's stories set in the Scottish Highlands and Islands. Remarkably two of these puffers were brought to Connemara and worked around the coast and islands, supplementing the established fleet of Galway hookers. We discussed our Scottish/Irish connections and experiences until suddenly the unpredictable O'Toole decided he was going to throw a large party in his newly-built house at Eyrephort on the Sky Road.

On the skite - Peter O'Toole, actor and hell raiser who loved Connemara.
Picture by the Daily Mail

I took it that it was to be 'a large party' because of the amount of drink this infamous hell-raiser ordered to take away with him. Again, if I recall rightly, cases of beer and bottles of wine and spirits were involved. His driver, who told me gleefully he was being paid by Peter to make a 100-mile round trip from Galway to Clifden twice a week to feed the O'Toole family cat, was kept busy stacking the booze into the boot of his car, which was parked outside in the square. It was with some reluctance that I declined to join him at the party since I had arranged earlier to meet up with some friends at a dance in Clifden Town Hall. Although Peter O'Toole himself was magnificent company – erudite, handsome and entertaining - the thought of spending the rest of the evening with his group of 'luvvies' didn't appeal all that much. I am afraid I wasn't star struck enough that night – or maybe my thoughts were with the black-haired, blue-eyed Galway girl I had a date with - although, with hindsight, I think that even though I was on holiday, I should have gone to the party. There was bound to be lots of eminently reportable gossip on the go and I contributed occasionally at the time to the William Hickey column in the *Daily Express*. The newspapers were desperate for celebrity stories – they still are - and I wasn't exactly flush with money.

One O'Toole story, which would have earned me some desperately needed money had I cottoned on earlier and sold it to the national press, was told to me later by Eoin King. It is repeated in Richard Murphy's autobiography, *The Kick.* O'Toole so admired the stone masonry work of John Cosgrove and Tom Coohill and the other Cleggan craftsmen who had built Richard Murphy's house at the pier that he engaged them to work on a new and much larger house for himself. Those others were Eoin King's brother in law, Paul Gordon, and Eoin Coyne, who also worked with Murphy, crewing the hookers; Brendan Coohill, Keiran Coneys and John Addley. O'Toole wanted his house to be built in the same pink granite stone as

Murphy's, but for it to be much bigger than the poet's house and to have more commanding views of the ocean. He wanted an outlook better even than the one from Robert Shaw and Mary Ure's much admired house in County Mayo. However, Galway County Council's planning officials insisted that the O'Toole house should be built neither on top of the hill nor at the foot of it but, inconveniently, behind it.

Determinedly the great actor went ahead with the construction even though the views of the ocean and the Slyne Head lighthouse were blocked out. He told everyone that he would, of course, comply with the planning laws in force at that time. However, mysteriously, one morning the hill obscuring his ocean view had disappeared. According to Richard Murphy's account of what happened Peter O'Toole 'got his builders to erect the house on the lower site and blast away the hilltop'. Eoin King's probably apocryphal account was less prosaic and a much better story. Eoin said O'Toole had commissioned the local battalion of the IRA to source the explosives and to blow up the hill. I think that was the story that O'Toole himself often related in his cups and that it is perhaps as accurate as the one about his name being Peter Seamus O'Toole, son of an Irish bookmaker and a Scottish nurse, and him being born in Clifden, Co Galway, Ireland.

Years later I was nominated as Columnist of the Year in the UK Press Gazette Awards and was invited to go to London to a presentation lunch at the Savoy Hotel. My bosses at Scottish and Universal Newspapers were so pleased that they allowed me to spend £100, a considerable sum at the time, on two guest tickets. I invited Paul Murphy, the Labour MP who later became the Secretary of State for Northern Ireland in the Blair government, and John McFall, an MP who later became chairman of the Treasury Select Committee at Westminster during the banking crisis, to be my guests. After the banking crisis, Tony Blair decided to send McFall to the House of Lords. Anyway, it was Ash Wednesday and the lunch got off to a bad start when McFall said he couldn't have much to eat and nothing at all to drink since he was a practising Catholic and it was a day of fasting from food and abstinence from alcohol. Paul Murphy said that since he was a Papal knight he would grant himself a dispensation and have a glass of white wine and a little salad. My disappointment - £50 for some lettuce and a glass of wine seemed a terrible waste of money - deepened when the moment came for the then Labour Party leader Neil Kinnock to announce the winners and present the awards.

I came second, which in most people's eyes, including my own, is nowhere. And then my guests made their excuses and left, scurrying back along The Strand and down Whitehall to Westminster to take part in a whipped vote in the House of Commons chamber at the ridiculously early time of 2.20pm.

And so the prospect loomed for a dull, disappointing and uneventful day until a few of the *Glasgow Herald* staff, including the editor, George McKechnie, award-winning writer Anne Simpson and reporter Stephen McGinty, who had won the award for Young Journalist of the Year, invited me to join them downstairs in the Coal Hole, the Savoy's public bar. With McGinty's award tucked away under his arm and a fat cheque in his wallet, we at last had something to celebrate. And celebrate we did in a manner for which Scottish journalists have a considerable reputation. Journalists have nothing to learn from MPs when it comes to fiddling their expenses. What started out as a swift gin and tonic extended into round after round of gins and tonic and pints of Guinness. The drinks were flying.

Lord Kinnock with Bill Heaney, Richard Harris portrait of the Bull McCabe from John B Keane's *The Field* in Hillary's at Leenane in Connemara and a poster of Peter O'Toole in the smash-hit move, *Lawrence of Arabia.*

Then, suddenly, on my way to the jacks, I heard this magnificent actorish voice booming out from a faraway corner of the Coal Hole. A large man in a sports jacket and open neck shirt, and with a silk scarf thrown carelessly about his neck, was presiding over a serious drinking session. The face was familiar. He had a pint of black stout gripped in his large right hand and had fully engaged a fascinated audience of barristers and clerks from the law courts on the opposite side of The Strand. Peter O'Toole? It couldn't be Peter O'Toole, not twice in the same lifetime, surely, or could it be? I walked across and said to him that I was sorry to interrupt – 'Peter O'Toole,' I said. 'I haven't seen you since we met in E J King's public house in Clifden in Connemara'. The big, blond fellow who was the target of my question looked up with a puzzled expression on his face. He was obviously annoyed at being interrupted. He said: 'Listen, I know E J King's bar and I love Connemara … but I am not Peter O'Toole.' I pulled back ever so slightly, but driven on by Dutch courage, I added: 'Ah, come on, you must remember. You were having a big party at your house that night. I think you were heading off to Oliver's in Cleggan to pick up some people before the start of it.' He looked for a moment as though he might hit me. And then he said: 'Look, I know Oliver's and I know Cleggan well, but I am not Peter O'Toole.' 'Very well then,' I said. 'If you don't want to talk to me then so be it.' And I made my way back to the bar and sat down with the *Glasgow Herald* crowd and some other journalists who were still drinking. Then Brian Hickey, a young *Herald* photographer, looked at me and said: 'I see you were talking to Richard Harris over there, Bill.' Such was my embarrassment, the ground could have opened up and swallowed me.

Richard Harris is of course linked to Connemara through his having starred as the Bull McCabe in the film of John B Keane's play, *The Field*. The black and white photographs taken on the set are still hanging above the turf fire at Hillary's public house in Leenane. A portrait of Harris hangs there too. John Hurt. Frances Tumelty and Brenda Fricker were in the cast of that film, produced by Jim Sheridan. My good friend Josephine DeCourcey from Cleggan is one of the many local people who took part as extras in that film which was made in and around Leenane and the Killary. Harris, of course, was also a regular member of O'Toole's notorious band of hell-raisers who include Richard Burton, Oliver Reed, Robert Shaw and anyone else who was up for finding out just how much punishment their liver could take in one session, or one session after another. Later, he swept out of the Coal Hole, drawing admiring glances from the women in the company and attracting everyone's attention to himself as only a great actor can. The assembled journalists, all of whom were by this time 'well on' chorused 'Bye Peter!' Somehow I don't think Richard Harris was amused that day.

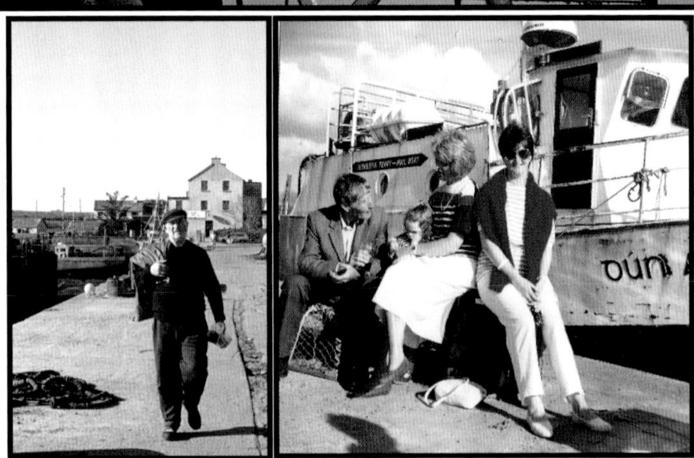

The Inishbofin ferry, Island of Discovery, heading for Cleggan Pier with skipper Pat Concannon in the wheelhouse; the late Paddy O'Halloran, who was the skipper of the old ferry, Dun Aengus, and Eoin King, Rosie and Gemma Woods and Bernie Heaney waiting till the boat comes in on Cleggan Pier. *Pictures by Bill Heaney*

Chapter 3
CLIFDEN BOOKSHOP

Poet Paul Durcan with Clifden Bookshop proprietors Maire O'Halloran and Nicole Shanahan during the Arts Festival. *Picture by Bill Heaney*

DOUBLE NEGATIVE
Richard Murphy

You were standing on the quay
Wondering who was the stranger on the mailboat
While I was on the mailboat
Wondering who was the stranger on the quay

Many years later, long after the Savoy Hotel incident, I met the poet Richard Murphy for a second time. I was in Connemara again, in Clifden for Arts Week, staying with my friend Dan Lynch and my brother-in-law Rodger Scullion as guests of John Sweeney at the Station House Hotel, and there were poets aplenty there. They included Michael Longley and Paul Durcan, both of whom gave readings of their work. Richard Murphy read some of his Cleggan poems, including *High Island* and *The Last Galway Hooker.* Richard Murphy was browsing in the Clifden Bookshop, a favourite spot owned and run by Nicole Shanahan and Maire O'Halloran, where I had just purchased a copy of his autobiography, *The Kick*, and I asked would he sign it for me. I told him who I was and double checked immediately who he was, confirming his identity as the Cleggan poet. I had met Murphy once, briefly in Joyce's public house, where he had been drinking with Sheddy Feeney, one of the last surviving

fisherman from the Cleggan Disaster of 1928, about which he wrote the famous eponymous poem. That meeting with Richard Harris in London had taught me a lesson I have never forgotten. Always double check not just that you have the correct name of the person that you are speaking with – but that you are talking to the person you think you are talking to. I told Richard Murphy that Eoin King, who had worked at his house on the pier, had died not long beforehand and he offered his condolences before writing: 'To Bill Heaney, a friend of Eoin King, with best wishes, Richard Murphy.' I still have that copy of the Murphy book, a remarkable memoir by a fine Celtic poet.
We all have embarrassing moments in our lives. My own most memorable, of course – or should that be forgettable? - was to confuse Richard Harris with Peter O'Toole. One of Richard Murphy's most forgettable moments was when Patrick Kavanagh conned him for ten shillings for drink in Dublin. By coincidence Kavanagh also appeared, if only in spirit, at Clifden Arts Week. His biographer, Antoinette Quinn, gave a well-attended talk on the Monaghan poet's life and times. Kavanagh too had suffered an embarrassing moment – and remarkably it involved Richard Murphy's wife, Patricia Avis, whose medical skills may have saved his life. Antoinette Quinn, in *Patrick Kavanagh: A Biography*, tells how in October, 1959, as the poet was making his way from Searson's pub in Upper Baggott Street in Dublin, he was almost drowned 'ironically in the stretch of canal near Baggott Street Bridge, which he had already celebrated in two sonnets'. Most of the people to whom Kavanagh related the circumstances of his plight believed he had staggered and fallen into the canal in the course of making the best of his way home after a night in the pub. Kavanagh himself was convinced however that someone had tried to murder him, an illustration that it is not just journalists who refuse to let the facts stand in the way of a good story. Whether he fell in or was pushed, the poet was lucky that the canal water was shallow and muddy enough to allow him to scramble to the bank and claw himself up it to safety. Kavanagh was fortunate too that remarkably he found himself outside the home of a friend – Patsy (Patricia) Avis Murphy. Patricia was a qualified doctor and although she never worked as a medical practitioner, she retained enough expertise to know how to deal with the shocked and muddy poet who turned up at her Wilton Place home at 1.30am. Thanks to Mrs Murphy's ministrations Kavanagh suffered no ill effects and was seen out and about in Parson's Bookshop and on his usual perambulations through the city later that day. He was wearing a splendid new tweed suit and a new watch, both purchased for him by Patsy Murphy, who was the daughter of a South African mining magnate and a wealthy woman in her own right.

Poets together, Richard Murphy (left) with Patrick Kavanagh.

It appears that since her split with Richard Murphy, Patsy Avis Murphy had set up home in Dublin where she became a patron of the arts, entertaining and supporting people like Kavanagh and Brian O'Nolan or Flann O'Brien, who wrote the Myles Na Gopaleen column for the *Irish Times.* O'Nolan was yet another Irish genius who was over fond of alcohol and eventually fell victim to it. In the end, Patrick Kavanagh never really lived down his most embarrassing moment. Indeed he made things worse for himself by mythologizing his recovery from his brush with death. He even portrayed himself in print as 'the man they couldn't kill'. But he had a message in his poetry for all of us who have had embarrassing moments such as I had with Richard Harris and who have lived to tell the tale when he wrote these lines in his poem *Dear Folks*:

The main thing is to continue,
To walk Parnassus right into the sunset
Detached in love where pygmies cannot pin you
To the ground like Gulliver. So good luck and cheers.

Poets are notoriously jealous of one another. Patrick Kavanagh, when asked by Patricia Avis Murphy what he thought of Richard Murphy's poetry, replied: 'Murphy has technique, but that's all, and it's not enough.' Patrick Kavanagh mentioned Connemara only once in these few lines from his poem, *The Paddiad*:

The party opens blub a blub
Paddy Whiskey, Rum and Gin
Paddy Three sheets on the wind;
Paddy of the Celtic Mist,
Paddy Connemara West ...

The Complete Poems of Patrick Kavanagh published by the Goldsmith Press. Richard Murphy's autobiography The Kick: A Life Among Writers is published by Granta.

Clockwise William Searson's public house in Upper Baggott Street; the Patrick Kavanagh bronze on a seat by the Grand Canal and the now closed Parson's Bookshop, where Kavanagh sat in the window, the house where Patrick Kavanagh lived in Dublin and another watering hole, The Waterloo. *Pictures by Bill and Bernadette Heaney*

Chapter 4
A STEP ALONG THE ROAD

Clifden in Connemara captured from the D'Arcy Monument. *Picture by Bill Heaney*

We had come across on the Burns Laird liner Scottish Coast from Glasgow to Dublin to see Glasgow Celtic playing against Shamrock Rovers in a friendly match at Dalymount Park in Dublin in August 1965. There were three of us – John Woods, Tom Moy and myself, and we were supposed to be in Ireland only for the football and only for the weekend. Celtic won the match 7-0 as expected and we went out afterwards into a few pubs and cafes in O'Connell Street, where we met up with three of the players from the squad who later won the European Cup in 1967, Lisbon Lions Jimmy Johnstone, Bobby Lennox and Charlie Gallagher. We had something to eat and a bit of a chat about the game before the footballers moved off in the direction of the Crystal Ballroom to become better acquainted with the Dublin talent. We had ourselves met some very personable young Scottish women on the boat over. They were, by remarkable coincidence, staying at the same digs as ourselves out in the sticks in Sutton and were planning to travel on the next morning to the Puck Fair at Killorglin in Co Kerry. We were intent on pursuing what we would have liked to have become our shipboard romances, and we wanted to see these young women again. To that end we headed off back to the guesthouse, where the girls were already, disappointingly, tucked up in bed. Mrs McCullough, the woman of the house, made it very clear there would be no hanky panky. The girls would not be getting up until breakfast time - and she would be patrolling the premises to ensure everyone would sleep undisturbed. So we were at a loose end and, as

everyone knows, the devil makes work for idle hands, especially the hands of young people on holiday.
John Woods said there was no possibility of us going with the Glasgow girls to Kerry. And, anyway, he wasn't attracted by the idea of heading off to a festival to honour a goat, even if its species had saved a whole village from attack centuries before. We should go and visit his aunt, he said. Was it far, we asked. No, it was 'just a step down the road' at Cleggan in Connemara. We would have to catch a train from Westland Row, he said, but it would be a dawdle and there were more pretty women there than you could shake a stick at. There would be dancing every night, plenty of Guinness and we would be able to afford it since we would have no digs to pay. For three young men in their early twenties this sounded just perfect. And it was ... when we got there eventually after a long train journey to Galway and an interminable bus ride from Galway to Clifden via Leenane and Letterfrack. Tom Moy had some idea of how far it would be. His mother, a Flaherty from Clifden, often spoke about Connemara. I remember her as an old lady who frequently delayed Tom's return to school after lunch by engaging him in a music *sessiun* in the house where she played the melodeon and Tom played the guitar. All the Moys were musical. Woodsie was a relation of mine, a second cousin. All my mother's cousins were Wards and his mother, Annie, was one of them. It was Annie's sister, Mary King, my Aunt Charlotte's best friend and sister-in-law, whose house we were heading for in Connemara.

Those were the days – left to right – John Woods and Tom Moy, Bill Heaney, Michael Anthony King and John Woods in the 'Sixties.

Twelve hours after leaving Dublin, we landed into Clifden. It was pitch dark. There were no buses for Cleggan and we had to drum up a taxi, which we did from Flanagan's the local undertaker's office. Mr Flanagan delivered us out in a limousine to the Pier Bar at Cleggan, where we met Eileen O'Malley for the first time and had a couple of pints before shouldering our cases and taking a hike out to Aughrusbeg. We arrived in to Mary King's about an hour later. It was like another world, a throw back in time. She was sitting by the turf fire. Her friend and neighbour, Maggie Cannon, was on the wooden settle bench under the window. It was a traditional, three room thatched Irish cottage, the likes of which we had only seen in *The Quiet Man*, complete with earthen floor in the main room. There were two very small bedrooms and we were allocated one of them with a big bed complete with a mattress of stitched together flour sacks filled with straw. There was just a tiny window looking out on to 'the street' at the front of the house, where there was a small hen house and a byre. Not only was there no 'en suite', there was no bathroom at all, no kitchen and no running water. And I don't think that Eoin King, Woodsie's cousin, was particularly delighted to see us since his mother had been unwell for some time with angina. Another group of Scottish relatives landing in on her and taking advantage of her house and good nature was all she needed, or didn't need in Eoin's opinion.

Eoin was the stay-at-home son, the youngest of three brothers and two sisters. His uncle, John Ward, was married to my grandfather's sister, Charlotte Heaney, who was best friend of his mother, who was John Ward's sister. John and Charlotte were witnesses at the marriage of my grandparents, William and Elizabeth (Healey) Heaney at St Joseph's Church in Helensburgh, Dunbartonshire, Scotland, before the First World War. Mary King was born in College Street, Dumbarton, of Connemara parents who had left Ireland after the Famine of the 1890s. Her father, also John Ward, who was born in Inishbofin, is said to have stolen a sheep and sold it to pay for a ticket on the emigrant boat from Westport or Sligo to Glasgow. He is reputed to have walked from Cleggan through the Mweelrea Mountains and Louisburgh to Westport via the Famine Road that runs up the side of the Killary Fjord and north through Doolough. When he got to Scotland, he headed for Dumbarton which had an excellent reputation with the immigrant Irish – Donegal writer Patrick MacGill, in one of his novels, states that one of his most famous characters, Moleskin Joe, was given a warm welcome and a bed there on his way to work as a navvy on the construction of the hydro-electric dams in Argyll and the West Highland railway line. John Ward secured employment in the shipyards and he and his wife provided lodgings in modest accommodation for a number of people from Connemara who came to Scotland in search of work. Mary, who was the youngest of their large family, worked in the bleach fields attached to the silk-dyeing works on the banks of the River Leven at Renton in Vale of Leven. My grandparents, Willie and Lizzie, remembered a disconsolate Mary King being sent to Connemara to look after her Murray grandparents, whom she had never met in her life before. Dumbarton was relatively prosperous at that time insofar as everyone who wanted to work had a job in the Clyde shipyards and factories or in the silk-dyeing industry which stretched from Renton to Balloch by Loch Lomond. Mary was heartbroken at having to leave her friends and brothers and sisters to travel to Ireland to look after the old folk in lovely but lonely Aughrusbeg, the back of beyond. I can only think from my own experience of having walked from Cleggan to Aughrusbeg on the dark night we three lads arrived there that Mary must have become more and more disconsolate as she walked that last mile or so. Connemara is not for the faint-hearted.

Bill Heaney looks across the lake at Aughrusbeg to the Wee Red Hoose.

Eventually, Mary Ward married Patrick King and the young couple and their family of five children, three girls and two boys, moved up in the world. Well, they moved 50 yards up into a tiny, thatched house at the top of a hill. Patrick, who was permanently in poor health, died eventually after long spells in hospital, and three of the children, John, Michael Anthony and Annie, emigrated to Scotland for work. The eldest child, Mary, became a nun in Liverpool and later Lisdoonvarna. Eoin, the youngest of the boys, stayed on at home to look after his mother and to eke out a living for both of them from the few cattle he kept in the hungry few acres the Congested Districts Board had allocated to the family at Aughrusbeg. Eventually, around 1970, Eoin built, with the help of friends and neighbours in what the Irish call a *meitheal,* a new house. Michael Anthony in England had 'sent home the slates' for the distinctive, now red-painted cottage to be built. Mary King lovingly named it Lakeview but, because of its Scottish links, this house became known to neighbours and friends as Scotch Corner or The Wee Red Hoose.

The house sits above a beautiful lake, which leaks out into the ocean at Aughrusmore. It appears on local maps as Lough Atalia. Otters swim there and cormorants fish from the rocks, corncrakes crekk and larks sing. Lone cuckoos calls out from the overhead telephone wires. The King residence looks out across boulder-strewn fields over the hamlet of Rosadillisk towards the snout of Cleggan Head; the island of Inishbofin and the Atlantic Ocean, next stop America, as they say frequently here. On a clear day you can see Clare Island and Croagh Patrick, St Patrick's Mountain, near Westport in Co Mayo. The name Aughrusbeg translates from Irish into English as Little Hunger. Aughrusmore (The Big Hunger) sits further west across the lake. Roundstone-based historian, author and naturalist, Tim Robinson, in his trilogy on Connemara, refers to Aughrusbeg as one of the places worst affected by the Great Famine of 1847. A report prepared for the Westminster Parliament, quoted on page 347 of the hard cover edition of Robinson's book *Connemara – listening to the wind*, states that the people occupying small cabins there were 'poor subtenants – most of them widows, forsaken wives, and young women carrying peat on their backs. They were nearly in a state of nudity, and appeared from actual want, to be reduced to a state of idiocy. There is no Irish animation and buoyancy here, but a stealthy and timid look, as if these poor souls were ashamed of their condition and lost to the faintest hope of escape from the wretchedness and misery …'

Tim Robinson's wonderful Connemara trilogy is published by Penguin.

Eighty years on, in 1928, that whole townland, plus the island of Inishbofin, was devastated by the Cleggan Disaster, about which you can read a detailed account, handed down by a survivor, elsewhere in this book. The writer and actor Walter Macken used the story and the setting of this disastrous incident for his novel *Rain on the Wind.* Connemara is also at the heart of Macken's trilogy, *Seek the Fair Land*, *The Silent People* and *The Scorching Wind.* Sadly, it was well into the middle of the 20th century before the people of Cushatrough, Emlough, Rosadillisk, Aughrusbeg, Aughrusmore and Sellerna began to emerge – although emerge they did and with great dignity, determination and commendable spirit – from the trials and sorrows which had beset them over the centuries since the cruel English general Oliver Cromwell banished the defeated Irish 'To Hell or Connacht'.

Anchor on the beach Beach at Aughrusbeg. Picture by Heather Greer

Clockwise are a turf stack at Marty and Geraldine Coyne's place at Rosadillisk; a donkey at Claddaghduff; Eoin King and friends at Claddaghdull Pony Show, and Lucy McEvilly of Cashel House Hotel on her Connemara pony.

Clockwise: Bunny Joyce enjoying the craic with the locals in his Cleggan public house; Connemara ponies brave the wind at Aughrus; Cleggan village approach from the west and the harbour at Cleggan, where the ferry leaves for Inishbofin.

Pictures by Bill Heaney

Chapter 5
KING'S RESIDENCE

Michael Anthony herds cattle outside the Kings' residence at Aughrusbeg, near Cleggan, in Connemara. *Picture by Bill Heaney*

And so it was that we three Scottish lads settled in to the King's residence. *We* loved that old cottage. It was a case of three in a bed and the little one said 'this is marvellous'. The fact that we had no bathroom and no running water was no inconvenience. It was a challenge, something to be enjoyed. Some of the young people who had been brought up in Connemara considered it a chore to have to walk half a mile for water. We looked upon it as an expedition which gave us a chance to get to know the place and the people. Who needed a bath when you could go for a swim in the Atlantic Ocean, which was just out the back of the house? I was such a poor swimmer that Eoin's big yellow dog, Tadgh, plunged into the sea after me to rescue me. My stroke was so poor that the dog appeared to believe that all the hashing and thrashing about I was doing was a prelude to me sinking without trace. We had a good laugh at that. That August in 1969 it was warm and sunny. There were cattle to be fed and milked and eggs to be collected. Sometimes the hens laid out in nettle beds in the fields at the back of the house. I went and helped Eoin to bring home turf from the bog. We stooked some of it in preparation for P J DeCourcey to come with his tractor and trailer which we helped to unload and stack in a neat pile at the side of the house.

Mary King made us a great feast that day and there were bottles of stout to wash it down – and whiskey for those who wanted it. We helped Mary with the chores and the cooking. She made her own soda bread in a pot sunk in red hot sods of turf and we learned how to 'hang down the kettle' over the fire which burned in the hearth night and day, 24/7 as they say nowadays. I used to smile when she asked me to 'hang down the kettle'. I had only ever hung anything up before, I told her. I had never hung anything down. And although they didn't speak much Irish in the King household, the words for everything that was small ended in 'een' as in teapoteen if she wanted the little teapot. I had been to Ireland many times before with my local Boys' Guild to their annual camps in places like Howth and Greystones and Wicklow. But this was different. This was Connemara and Connemara is the real Ireland, the Ireland of J M Synge's *Riders to Sea* and *The Playboy of the Western World.* The Connemara made famous by Walter Macken, author, actor and playwright from Galway.

Eoin and Michael Anthony King working on the lazy beds at Aughrusbeg.
Picture by Bill Heaney

We snagged turnip and pulled potatoes in the lazy beds. We attended the Cleggan regatta and danced to the ceilidh band there. We went swimming with the Yanks who were staying 'below' at Marty's house. We had boiled eggs at Honey's two-storey house down by St Brigid's strand and we drummed up and ate the mussels and whelks we picked from the Rosadillisk rocks. We went to the beach barefoot to catch flounders or 'flook', which we speared with a hayfork and had for our tea. And we went to the dancing in Clifden, Letterfrack and Ballyconneely. We sang in Sweeney's Strand Bar in Claddaghduff with Sean and Ellie O'Toole. Sean played the accordion and Ellie was a wonderful singer. They are both long since passed away, God rest them, but fortunately Sean and Ellie's children and grandchildren have inherited their musical talents. I'll bet there are still memorable parties at the O'Toole house in Claddaghduff. We would go to Bunny and Ulick Joyce's pub in Cleggan where we would also have a sing song or a 'sessiun' and from there to Oliver's and the Pier Bar. There was no thought ever of going home. I remember being offered the chance to take cattle to the fair in Clifden. Eoin King said

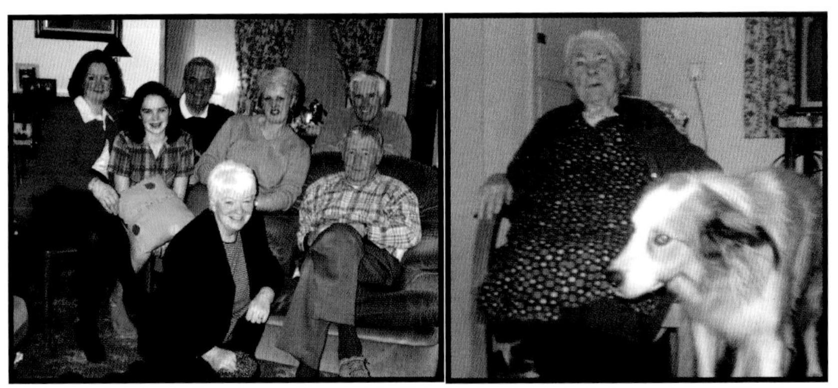

Relaxing at home (left to right) Bernie Heaney, Gemma Woods, Bill Heaney, Rosie Woods, Terry McWilliams and Eoin King with Margaret Woods McWilliams in front.
Pictures by Stephen Woods and Bill Heaney

it was unlikely that I would make it if I went out the night before. But out I went – and I did make it. It's the first and only time in my life I have had my breakfast before I went to bed. Mary King had tea and toast and eggs ready when we got home from the dancing at one o'clock in the morning. We ate up and got up – at 2.30am. The task at hand was to take four cattle to Clifden and sell them at the fair which took place on the street. There was no cattle market in those days. John Sweeney and Malachy King were yet to embark on that venture in Clifden. Inevitably it rained … and it rained … and it rained. We teamed up with Robin Lacey, a neighbour who was then the proud owner of a blue Ford Anglia. Robin decided it would be a good idea to take the car. We could all take turns inside it to shelter from the rain. He would drive the car and we would drive the cattle, which we did all the way into Clifden. We set out just after 3am and walked slowly over the mountain to where the road branches off for Westport. The water was running out of us. We were soaked through and the cattle were awkward and frisky. Sometimes they jumped off the road into fields and we had to roust them out of it and back on to the road. And then we met the first of the jobbers, the men whose job it was to buy cattle for the big farmers who would take them and finish them off in the lush grazing of their farms near Dublin before finally taking them to the boats for the lucrative beef export trade to Britain and France. I was delighted when Eoin told me who these men were. I thought he would soon sell the cattle and we would be off in Robin's Ford Anglia and back to our beds. Little did I know how these things worked. I hadn't a clue about custom and practice. The first approaches from the jobbers were brusquely rebuffed. There was no way we would sell at that price, Eoin told them. And so we kept walking and walking and it kept raining … and raining. On we went along past the cut off for Streamstown and past Shanaheever and over the hill and down the shortcut past St Anne's old people's home to St Joseph's Catholic Church. We were in Clifden at last. The cattle would be sold soon, I hoped, and we could go home. No such luck. We herded Robin Lacey's four and our three up against the wall past the chapel and Eoin went walkabout. The town filled up. The hours passed. We went into a shop for something to eat for our breakfast. I could hardly keep my eyes open for my second breakfast of the day.

Back we went then to the cattle and the fascinating business of buying and selling. The owners talked to the buyers incessantly and at such a speed I could hardly understand a word they were saying. They discussed everything but the price of the cattle. Why don't they just come to an agreement, hand over the money and let us get out of here, I wondered. The air was pungent with the almost over-powering smell of newly-dropped dung. It was on our boots and our clothing and then the sun came out and the steam rose up from our coats and jackets as they began to dry out. Eoin went walkabout again.

Bill Heaney walked the cattle to Clifden in the middle of the night.

A large tourist bus drove into town and all these Americans got out to watch the serious business that looked to them like fun and games. I had an old tweed hat of Eoin's on my head and an ancient coat tied at the waist with a rope. The tourists obviously thought I was fair game for a photograph and their cameras came out. I was almost sleeping on my feet by this time. The steeple clock chimed on the church on the hill. Late arrivals landed into town where all was chaos and the traffic was unable to move. Not much was moving on the sales front either. Eoin had said he wanted £40 for each of the cattle we had. If anyone approached me with that kind of money then I was to fetch him immediately and he would complete the deal. And we could go home. The jobbers knew I was a rookie – and they don't deal with rookies. Where was himself, they asked. I had no idea where he was, which public house he was in now. People were spilling out of the pubs on to the streets. Others were pushing their way in and calling for drink. Jobbers and farmers were shaking hands, spitting on hands and handing out luckpennys. I was rooted to the spot, rigid, greatly regretting not having gone to my bed at a decent hour the night before and being stupid enough to have that one last pint in Joyce's. Then Eoin came back. One of the jobbers, whom he knew by name, came up and offered his 'three forties' – the magic £120. But he didn't take it. They went on about the luckpenny. I think Eoin wanted a £2 luckpenny for each beast. The jobber walked away and I thought he was gone for good. I had visions of having to walk the five miles back to Cleggan. I said to him 'For God's sake, Eoin, take the money. I'll give you the £6 to make up the difference. Never mind the luckpenny.' But he said No, there would be no question of that. It was a matter of professional pride. He would get the price he was looking for or the jobbers could take a hike. 'It's us who'll be taking the hike,' I thought to myself, 'all the way back to Cleggan.' And so it was that we set out on the return journey home in deep despair. I thought I was going to die from the effects of the hangover, the lack of sleep, the heat of the sun, the wet clothing and pure exhaustion. We were making our way up the hill past the chapel when the trench-coated jobber jumped out and put his mark on each of Eoin's cattle. I could have kissed that jobber, big and ugly as he was. We took the jobber's paper chit, said our farewells to the much loved, well-minded cattle, each of whom had a name, and headed back into town where we cashed in at the bank and went for something to eat with the other Cleggan farmers, who were well into their lunch by this time. I sat down on a chair, my head dropped on to the table immediately and I fell fast asleep. Dickie Davis gave us a lift back to Aughrusbeg in his over-packed car if I remember rightly. I was never so happy to get to my bed in all of my life. That fantastic football weekend in Ireland lasted a month or more. I loved Connemara so much that I wanted to stay there forever. We kept on going until our money ran out.

Cattle forage amongst the boulders at Aughrusbeg in Connemara.

To Hell or Connacht – the boulder strewn land at Aughrusbeg where Oliver Cromwell expected banished Connemara families to eke out a living.

My colleagues on the news agency where I worked at the time sent me money to get me home again. They say that in life it's a good idea to look back – but not to go back. I don't believe that for a moment. I was very sad to leave Cleggan though and for many years since I have gone back to Connemara again and again. Even in my dreams. It is to Connemara that the words of this poem by James Clarence Mangan transport me:

I walked entranced
Through a land of Morn;
The sun with wondrous excess of light
Shone down and glanced
Over seas of corn
And lustrous gardens aleft and right ...

Some years later, long after that first day at the fair in Clifden, Eoin King once again asked me if I would like to help him to sell some cattle. I was a happy man when I found out that John Sweeney and Malachy King had built a new and modern livestock market on the Galway Road in Clifden. John would be sending a lorry and drovers round to collect the cattle in question. We would be travelling by car, thanks be to God.

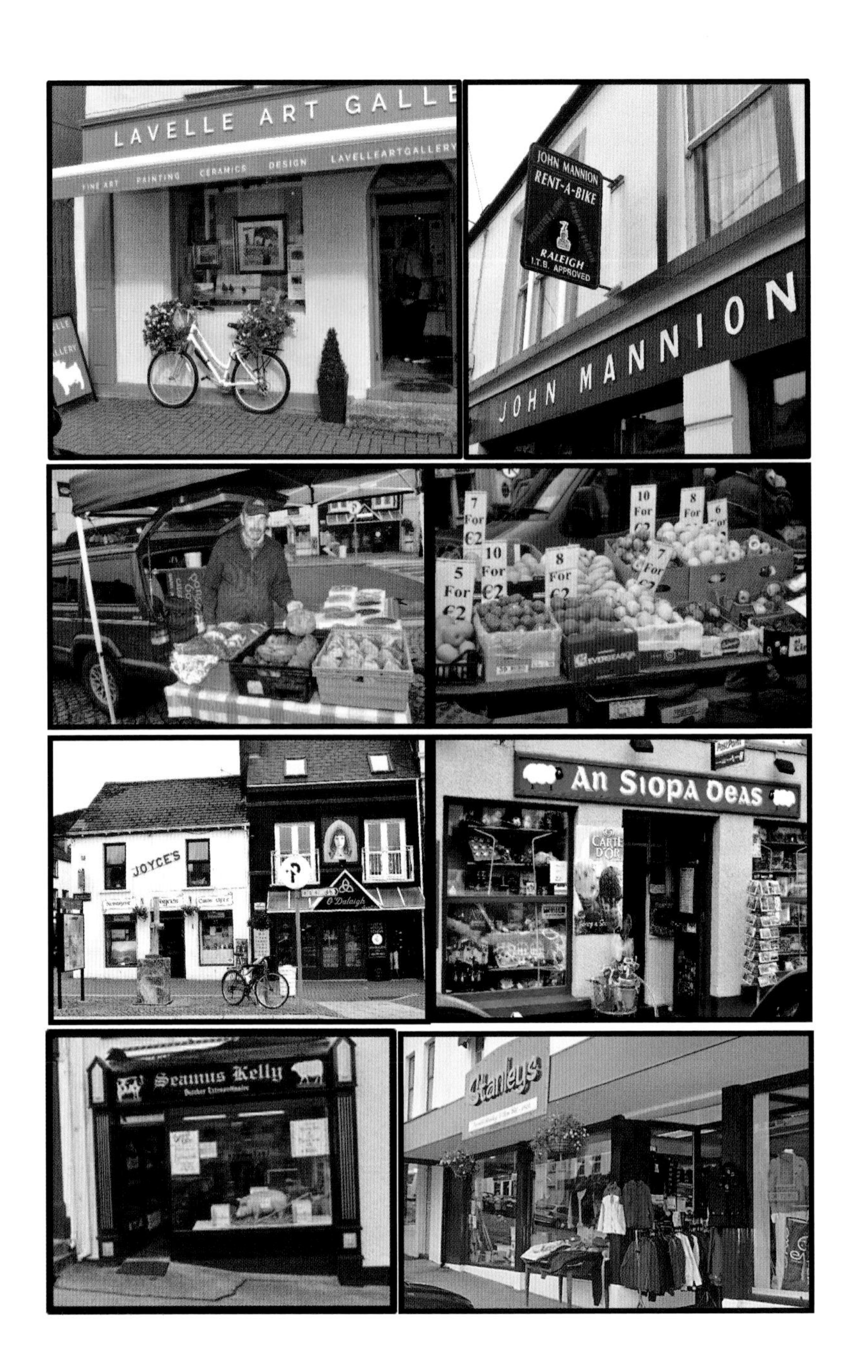
LAVELLE ART GALLE
FINE ART PAINTING CERAMICS DESIGN LAVELLEARTGALLERY
JOHN MANNION
RENT-A-BIKE
RALEIGH
I.T.B. APPROVED
JOHN MANNION
7 For €2
10 For €2
8 For
6 For
5 For €2
10 For €2
8 For €2
7 For €2
JOYCE'S
O'Dalaigh
An Siopa Deas
Seamus Kelly
Stanleys

Clifden, the capital of Connemara, is colourful and busy and a place where you can buy almost anything from fresh bread from the tail-gate of Letterfrack man John Walsh's estate wagon to fresh fruit at the street market to an Aran gansey at Percy Stanley's, a bucket and spade for the beach or a postcard at *An Siopa Deas* to send home, sausages or a steak at Seamus Kelly's butcher shop, a beautiful painting or print at Lavelle's or just enjoy a steaming bowl of fish chowder and a pint of Guinness at E.J. King's or one of the many restaurants, hotels and public houses in Main Street and Market Street. You can hire a bike at Mannion's in Bridge Street. The Alcock and Brown Hotel in Market Square; Lowry's bar and traditional music house and Vaughan's excellent public house.

Clockwise: The colourful Main Street in Clifden; the excellent Marconi Restaurant; Guinness at Griffin's in Main Street; The Derryclare pizza house, Tom King's B and Boylesports betting shop; Vaughan's menu and Mannion's Bar in Market Street.

Pictures by Bill Heaney

Chapter 6
LOUIS MACNEICE

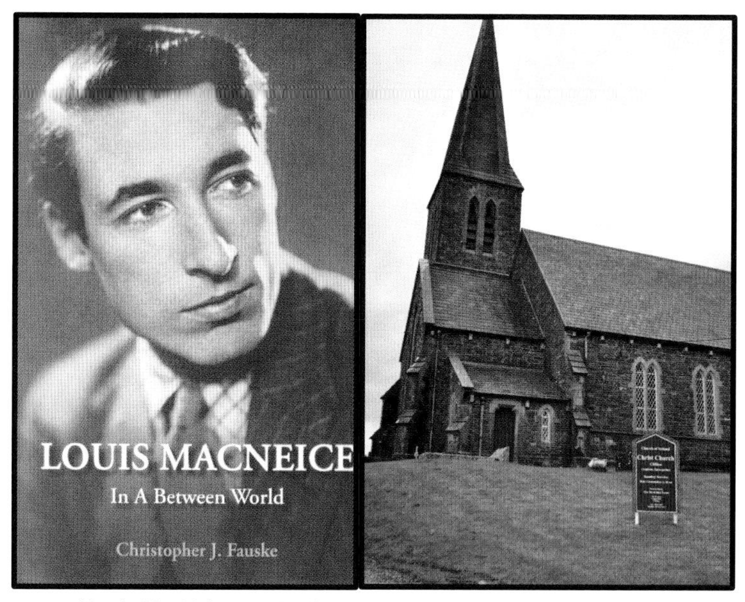

Louis MacNeice, the Belfast poet, and Christ Church, Clifden.

There is a fine black and white photograph of Richard Murphy's Galway hooker *Ave Maria* in full sail off the Connemara island of Inishbofin. It is included in Jon Stallworthy's biography of the Belfast poet Louis MacNeice, whose father was born in Omey Island. Murphy's red-sailed pookaun, a smaller version of a hooker, is also in the photograph sailing along in her wake. Louis MacNeice and his wife, Bimba, visited the West of Ireland in 1962 on his way to speak at the Yeats International Summer School in Sligo. Stallworthy states that 'the high point of this happy expedition was their visit to the poet Richard Murphy' in Cleggan, where he took them for a sail. What is surprising about this is that Murphy and MacNeice were on friendly terms at all because MacNeice, who worked at the BBC in London, had rejected Murphy's '*Voyage to an Island*' for broadcasting on radio. Recalling in his autobiography how he had been in London in exalted company, including Cecil Day-Lewis in 1953, Murphy said MacNeice had rejected his 'long-winded epic' and that he had unnerved him when they met by declaring 'The West of Ireland is finished.' Murphy recalled meeting him in a pub near the BBC called The Stag – 'he was wearing a green tweed suit and a bow tie, and he kept turning his eyes to the door to see who was entering.'

There appears to have been little genuine warmth between Murphy and MacNeice, but they shared a common heritage in Connemara. Both their grandfathers were linked to the Church of Ireland in the parish of Clifden and Omey. And now, many years later, here were their progeny drinking and socialising together in Eileen O'Malley's Pier Bar at Cleggan. Murphy may have been resident in Connemara, but MacNeice can claim to have stronger connections since his father was actually born in Omey Island, off Claddaghduff. Omey was a place to which Murphy went often. It can be reached by walking across half a mile of strand when the Atlantic tide is out. St Feichin's monastery of the seventh century has long been buried under the sand there and it is home to the local cemetery. Funerals from Our Lady Star of the Sea, the Catholic chapel in Claddaghduff, have to take place according to the tides so that the cortege and the mourners can travel safely into the island across a causeway. In the past, half a dozen pall bearers would simply shoulder the coffin and walk to the graveyard, often in the most appalling weather, to complete the committal service.

Richard Murphy's Galway hooker *Ave Maria* in full sail off the Connemara island of Inishbofin. Murphy's red-sailed pookaun, a smaller version of a hooker, is also in the photograph sailing along in her wake.

That edge between the two poets comes through in a passage in Murphy's biography when he goes out of his way to make it clear that his grandfather, Canon Richard Murphy, who was Rector of Clifden in the parish of Omey from 1904 until his death in 1916, never proselytised or helped the Irish Church Missions, which operated in Omey and Aughrus, to do so – 'and he kept on good terms with the Catholic priest.' MacNeice's grandfather, William, however, decided early in life to be a schoolmaster with the ICM and to take the Protestant faith to Roman Catholics. The aim of such schools was to convert the children of the frequently starving peasantry and, offering them food, clothes and a better education than the Catholic hedge schools. They were fairly successful -- although quite a number of converts subsequently reverted back to the faith of their fathers.

Horse racing on the strand between Omey Island and Claddaghduff.

Picture by Heather Greer

It was little wonder that many of the islanders on Omey 'took the soup'. An American evangelist who had visited the island said the miseries of overcrowding and poverty there had to be seen to be believed. However what happened in the end was that the missionaries and their family were run out of Omey. This is said to have happened after a clash between the Catholic curate and William MacNeice. And that in the stramash that followed the curate was hit over the head with a soup ladle. A woman who was accidentally shot in the uproar that followed died some years later from her injuries. Richard Murphy says not even a stone remains of the Protestant 'soup school' and schoolmaster's house, where Louis MacNeice's father, Fred, who became a Church of Ireland rector himself and, eventually, a bishop, was born. The MacNeice family eventually took up residence in Belfast, where the poet himself was born, an event he recalls in his brilliant poem *Carrickfergus*:

I was born in Belfast between the mountain and the gantries
To the hooting of lost sirens and the clang of trams.

The Omey of today is a very different place from it was in those turbulent years around the time of the Famine. Its 500 acres are a haven for ramblers and or riding and swimming and boating. In the middle of the 19th century the number of people living there matched exactly the number of acres – 500. The women and children occupied the poorest of cabins. That poverty extended well into the 20th century but it is now thankfully gone as have nearly all of the population. Only a few people live there permanently now. However, in summer months there is a lot happening around Omey and Claddaghduff, including the Claddaghduff Pony Show and Omey Races, which are held on the strand. The sound of traditional music can be heard around Sweeney's Strand Bar where there are regular *sessiuns* and nearly every day riders from Cleggan take their horses for exercise on to the sands.

But back to MacNeice himself. My own favourite of all his poems is *Bagpipe Music,* which I suppose isn't surprising for a Scotsman, which includes the following lines:

It's no go the merry go round, it's no go the rickshaw,
All we want is a limousine and a ticket for the peepshow.

Meanwhile, a new MacNeice biography by Professor Christopher J Fauske has been published by the Irish Academic Press. *In Between World* offers a powerful new perspective on MacNeice's life and work. Fauske places the poet's relationship with Ireland, the Second World War, his father and the key women in his life at its centre. The biography explores the Irish and British social, political and religious contexts in which the poet's life was rooted. It deals with his unstable upbringing, ill-defined nationality and tempestuous love life. His wide experience and interest shaped a body of work that was both affirming of life and deeply uncertain about anyone who claimed to have its answers. This is a fastidious book that pays long-overdue heed to MacNeice's heroic directive: 'Let every adverse force converge.'

Louis MacNeice by Jon Stallworthy is published by Faber and Faber in London
and In A Between World by the Irish Academic Press in Dublin

A typical Connemara cottage in a beautiful setting near Omey Island at Aughrusmore, home of Fergus and Mary Rose Cahill, both of whom were attached to *The Chieftains* traditional music legends. *Picture by Bill Heaney*

Chapter 7
McGAHERN LOVED CLEGGAN

John McGahern's *Memoir* published by Faber and Faber.

John McGahern is the author of six highly acclaimed novels and four collections of short stories. He has been compared to Chekhov and Proust and was the recipient of many awards and honours, including the Society of Authors, the American-Irish Award, the Prix Ettrangere Ecureuil and the Chevalier de l'Ordre des Arts et des Lettres. His work has appeared in anthologies and has been translated into many languages and, according to his *Memoir*, he was intent in settling down in Connemara until his wife, Madeline, said she would prefer to live in the Leitrim countryside where her husband was brought up rather than near the sea.

In that memoir, McGahern tells how, after having become divorced from his Finnish wife Annikki, he had met Madeline and they had travelled together to America where he had been offered a visiting professorship. When they returned to Europe, they lived in Paris for a time before returning to Ireland. They found a house near Clifden – 'We made friends, we had drinks with our neighbours in the local bars, we walked or cycled everywhere, and it was easy to get lifts. On more ambitious outings, we took the bus to Galway. I was given the use of a boat and started to fish on the ocean.' McGahern and Madeline stayed at first as guests of Richard Murphy in the pink granite New Forge near the pier. The couple then got a house about a mile west of the village. The author tells how he went fishing with Patrick O'Malley, the Cleggan postman and farmer, and how sometimes they went to late-night music sessions in the Renvyle Hotel – 'I had a small contract to supply the Renvyle whenever we had a surplus of fresh mackerel. No money ever changed hands, but we had a small account in the bar and restaurant.' At the sessions, John and Patrick often met up with Father Gibbons, who was the priest on Inishbofin 'with a beautiful singing voice'. They became good friends and on one occasion he travelled to Leitrim with him to meet his father. The author tells how the summer that year in

Cleggan was warm and dry and the Irish army had pitched tents above the strand for military exercises. 'We danced at a marquee that was erected in the middle of the village for a whole week,' he recalled.

McGahern enjoyed the social life in Cleggan such, as the entertainment supplied by this ceilidh band on the pier on Regatta Day. *Picture by Bill Heaney*

John McGahern and Patrick O'Malley had lobster pots and nets as well as lines for the fishing. McGahern tells how he caught lobsters and crayfish 'and plenty of crab, some salmon and sea trout as well as the usual pollack and mackerel, mullet and rock fish'. They sold some of the fish, took visitors out on the boat on fishing trips and occasionally went out on trips to Inishbofin – 'This was hazardous except in calm weather. When the boat engine overheated, it stopped and all that could be done was to let it drift until the engine cooled.' John McGahern, as well as fishing, often went to work on the bog cutting turf with Patrick O'Malley whom he says was 'intelligent and proud, quick and generous, but also extremely competitive'. I can vouch for the fact that Patrick had a sharp mind. I took off one afternoon on Eoin King's bicycle for a trip around Aughrus Point and, inevitably, stopped off for a pint and some Connemara conversation at Sweeney's Strand Bar in Claddaghduff. Patrick was in the bar with a few locals and I was invited as usual to join in their discussion about politics. My Socialist slip soon began to show and Patrick's memorable comment when he thought I had over-stepped the mark was: 'That lad's from the Bernadette Devlin School of Politics.' I wore that remark as a badge of honour forever after. What I do know about Patrick is that he would have made a very good councillor or TD and that he was that he was always very keen to do anything that would help to bring work and prosperity to Connemara. Patrick and his family have certainly done that with a number of extremely successful projects linked to tourism and fishing.

Clockwise: Paul pours a pint of stout at Sweeney's Strand Bar in Claddaghduff; a piebald foal at Rosadillisk, and Sweeney's petrol station, shop and bar.
Pictures by Bill Heaney and Heather Greer

Where Patrick did not have any success however was in talking John McGahern into staying permanently in Cleggan. He earmarked a suitable house for the author and tried to talk him into buying it, but Madeline said no. McGahern writes: 'I would have been happy to have stayed in Cleggan, and would have made my way. I was as drawn to the ocean as I was once drawn to the river in Oakport.'

After McGahern died in 2006, the writer Joseph O'Connor paid him this deserved tribute: 'I was introduced to John McGahern's short stories as a teenager by my parents. I can still remember the first time I read *Sierra Leone*. The sentences in that story were so simple and forceful that they made me wonder what it was like to write them. 'Her hair shone dark-blue in the light' was one of them. The strange ache in the heart caused by quiet, precise words.

'Later I discovered his bleak, spare novels: *The Barracks, The Dark, The Pornographer,* and then *Amongst Women*, the most important Irish novel of the late 20th century. The magnificent short stories continued to come. The last piece in his Collected Stories (1992), a jewel called *The Creamery Manager*, is one of the finest short stories imaginable, a model of understated power. It rivals James Joyce's *The Dead.*

'Readers will remember John McGahern as a writer whose work touched them, or changed their point of view, casting light into the everyday corners. Literary fashions came and went; he ignored all of them, absolutely. He was a writer whose work resonated in whatever part of our souls needs to be touched by beauty. You read McGahern and you said, 'that's true'.

'Like [Seamus] Heaney, or Patrick Kavanagh, or Raymond Carver, or Joyce, he was able to take the stuff of ordinary lives and create of it the highest art. This is why his books were so frequently best-sellers in his native Ireland. His work spoke to readers about their own lives; its silences were also ours. It crackled with a kind of hopefulness, though it offered no tricks. Integrity and a sense of place cohere in his writing; his way of looking at the world was unique. This, he always stressed, was the most important thing the writer needs to find. Not a voice alone, not the words alone, but a way of seeing into lives.

'McGahern was an exceptionally modest man, but his standards were the highest. There were often many years between his books. He was one of the very few Irish writers of recent decades who only published masterpieces.'

Clockwise from top are Josephine DeCourcey and guests from Scotland and France on her Sunday night Connemara FM radio show; Newman's Bar, which is famed for its music; an impromtu session at Olivers in Cleggan; Fresh fish sign at King's in Cleggan; Oonagh pours a pint at the Pier Bar in Cleggan and more music at Olivers'.

Pictures by Bill Heaney and Heather Greer

Chapter 8
THE FRENCH CONNECTION

President Charles De Gaulle of France with President Eamon De Valera of the Republic of Ireland.
Picture by Irish Times

Two French generals made a huge impact on the West of Ireland. They were General De Gaulle, who came to Connemara on holiday for two weeks in 1969, and General Humbert, who came to support the United Irishmen and made a vain attempt to drive out the English in 1798, which inevitably has become known as The Year of the French. General De Gaulle was a man who settled only for the best, not only in politics but in life. He once said: 'Aim high, win or lose, but never settle for mediocrity.'

When he came to Connemara he knew he would get only the best. He sought peace and quiet from the stresses and strains of guiding his country through the complex business of uniting the major countries of Europe to become an economic community. One is left wondering what he would have thought of the UK Referendum result in the United Kingdom in 2016. General and Madame De Gaulle succeeded in their quest for the sanctuary and sybaritic comfort of the beautiful house and gardens at Cashel House Hotel, where the former British Prime Minister Harold Macmillan had also stayed on holiday with his wife, Lady Dorothy. General De Gaulle's substantial contribution to Connemara was that his visit was widely publicised and it attracted people from across the world to visit Connemara. French people make up a large proportion of the visitors who come to the West of Ireland to this day.

Cashel House was designed and built in 1840 for Captain Thomas Hazell. The Hazells were English landowners and were also agents for a Scottish company buying kelp – a type of seaweed, which is used in the manufacture of toothpaste and other alginate-based products. The old kelp store still stands by the pier opposite Doon House. Captain Hazell and his wife celebrated their 40th wedding anniversary at Cashel House in 1885. The rose hedge outside the hotel bar is said to be his present to her on that occasion. Mrs Hazell laid out the gardens and planted many of the flowering shrubs and trees which are such an attraction today.

Dermot and Kay McEvilly purchased Cashel House in 1967. Total refurbishment began immediately, with a fine collection of antiques being added and offering all modern facilities.

The house reopened in May, 1968, and is still owned by the same family. A year later, General and Madame De Gaulle spent a memorable two weeks there. General Humbert, who landed with his troops at Kilcummin in Co Mayo, was less fortunate. Although he won a number of battles, most memorably at Collooney and Castlebar, the insurrection he supported was brutally crushed and his soldiers and rebel army sent homeward to think again. 'Homeward' for many of them was the Twelve Pins of Connemara, where they found themselves constantly pursued and hunted down by the English. However, many of the troops escaped or were smuggled to freedom in France The most notable of these rebels, Father Myles Prendergast, an Augustinian friar from Murrisk in Co Mayo, who had for years been an ardent supporter of the United Irishmen, and who had rushed to welcome General Humber to Castlebar, came eventually to live in Clifden. He had made a daring escape from prison in Castlebar with two members of the Gibbons family, Johnny and Affy, who were first cousins. Johnny Gibbons' father was Lord Altamont's land agent, who eventually became treasurer of the Connacht branch of the United Irishmen.

River deep, mountain high in the countryside at Cashel where President De Gaulle loved to walk, a peaceful paradise for anglers and hill walkers. *Picture by Bill Heaney*

Stories about the exploits of Father Miley abound still in Connemara and some of these are recounted by Tim Robinson is his book *Connemara: The Last Pool of Darkness.* When the rebellion was suppressed he went on the run and became leader of the Connemara outlaws whose priority was to escape falling into the clutches of Denis Browne, brother of Lord Altamont of Westport House, who was the chief prosecutor and indeed persecutor of the United Irishmen. Robinson says Browne went about his task with such enthusiasm that he earned the nickname of Soap-the-Rope. Affy Gibbons is said to have avoided capture by fleeing to Inishbofin where he got work as a teacher – 'but quarrelled with one of the Coneyses in a drinking house there and was murdered'. Johnny Gibbons and Father Miley were more fortunate – for a time. Although he was caught and put into jail in Galway, Gibbons escaped and teamed up with Valentine Jordan, an important rebel leader who had returned from exile in France to join the Connemara outlaws. Johnny Gibbons' life came to an end at the end of a rope however when two women soaked his pistols in water and informed the redcoats of his whereabouts. He was delivered into the hands of Soap-the-Rope's men and bundled up to the scaffold where he cried out: 'Ah, Connemara, my five hundred farewells to you; no treachery would have come to me had I stayed with you.' After many years of living on the run, Lord Mayo is said to have negotiated a pardon for Father Miley, who gave up the priesthood and lived into the 1840s in a cottage south of Ballinaboy. He lived by playing the bagpipes at weddings and used to write out excerpts from the gospels for people to wear around their necks as a charm.

Not only presidents, poets, film stars and fishermen enjoyed their holidays in Connemara. The editor's sons, Bryan and Damian Heaney, loved it too.

Chapter 9
A FLOCK OF WINDY ISLANDS

The harbour on a fine day at Inishbofin Island off Cleggan in Connemara.
Picture by Peter Walsh

Why come to Connemara? There are many reasons but the most quoted ones are the diverse landscapes, scenic mountain walks, long, sandy beaches, first class sea and river fishing and the fascinating history going back to the time of Cromwell. Connemara is an enigma. It is neither a province nor a county and it has no administrative status and no marked boundaries. It is made up of the western portion of County Galway, between Lough Corrib, and the wild Atlantic shore. And it includes offshore islands, some of which are still inhabited. To the north in Co Mayo is the nine-mile-long Killary Fjord, so called because it is so deep and narrow that it would not look out of place in Norway. To the south and west Irish is spoken in what's called the Gaeltacht, but in Clifden the main language is English. It is without question the remarkable diversity of landscapes and weather, and the warmth of the people who live here, that draws people to Connemara. And brings them back time and time again. The people live mostly in small farms in townlands in new houses and bungalows which have replaced the old thatched cottages and cabins. The rivers are deep and the mountains are high. There are three mountain ranges – Mweelrea in South Mayo, the Partry Mountains and the Twelve Pins. None of the mountains is higher than 3,000 feet however and there is good access to them for walking and climbing. There are good roads for people who like to go out in the car for a day and drive around the place or, better still and better for them, going round on a bicycle.

There is too what the poet Austin Clarke called 'a flock of windy islands' which can be reached by good ferry services, particularly from Cleggan to Inishbofin. The weather is a big thing here. There can be four seasons in one day, sun, rain, hail and snow. But it's something you will get used to and come in time to look forward to. Some parts of Connemara are pretty wet, or wet and pretty if you like, receiving up to 225 days of rain per year, but the climate in Connemara is as variable as the landscape. May can be hot and dry, August chilly and damp, but a typical day in Connemara is more likely to provide a bit of everything. One respected travel writer wrote: 'Whatever conditions you encounter, it's hard to return from Connemara without a healthy, weather-beaten glow.'

There is huntin', fishin' and shootin' aplenty in Connemara, and there is horse riding and pony-trekking too. Walking and cycling are major here and off the roads there is in Connemara National Park a purpose-built walkway which runs for 3.5km to the top of Diamond Hill. From up there walkers can feast their eyes on magnificent views of the west coast and the scattering of islands beyond it. As well as mountain walks, the national park has gentler nature trails through its grassland and woodland, some of them guided. There's an exhibition centre and café at the heart of the complex, which opens 10am-5.30pm throughout the year, closing an hour later in June, July and August. Admission and the guided walks are free. You can hire a bike at Mannion's in Bridge Street, Clifden, and in most of the bigger villages and towns. Cyclists relish the quiet, twisting roads and if you are fit enough to tackle a few stiff climbs then take the Sky Road. That is so much worth seeing. Golfers will love the championship links of Connemara Golf Club at Ballyconneely – some of the bounces off the fairways can be very interesting indeed - and there are opportunities to go boating, swimming and snorkeling. One remarkable island worth visiting is Inishbofin, which can be accessed by ferry from Cleggan, where the pier was built in 1822 by the Scottish civil engineer Alexander Nimmo. Clifden historian Kathleen Villiers-Tuthill has written a book about Nimmo's civil engineering achievements. There were plans to build an airport at Cleggan which must have been one of the first parts of Ireland to have been spotted by aviators Alcock and Brown on their historic transatlantic flight from Newfoundland in 1919, but these have been shelved. Keep your feet on the ground – or better still on the decks of the *Island Discovery* with skipper Pat Concannon and his crew on the Inishbofin ferry. There are good hotels and excellent walks on Inishbofin which is steeped in history. Chill out by its peaceful loughs, watch birds by the rugged cliffs or go swimming on the secluded sandy beaches.

There are two colonies of seals, and amongst the rare birds that breed here is the elusive, endangered corncrake or landrail, as that bird is sometimes called. You'll hear the call of the cuckoo and the song of the lark on warm summer days there. The corncrake's 'crekk, crekk' can be heard coming from the low lying meadows, where some of the hay is still cut by hand or left uncut till very late in the season. Inishbofin is also known for its traditional music, affinity with poets and poetry and the visitor amenities are excellent, with a range of bed and breakfast and self-catering accommodation.

Clockwise: Fish merchant Johnny King boxes newly-landed mackerel at Cleggan Pier; three men in a currach in Cleggan Bay; Noreen Higgins of Oliver's bar and restaurant; Josephine DeCourcey's Hazelwood guesthouse above Cleggan Pier; West Atlantic Way sign for Inishbofin and a view of Oliver's from Cleggan Pier. *Pictures by Bill Heaney*

Paddy O'Halloran in the cap sees a party of visitors off from Cleggan Pier to Inishbofin on board the old Dun Aengus.

The Island Discovery heading towards Cleggan from Inishbofin with skipper Pat Concannon at the helm. *Picture by Bill Heaney*

Chapter 10
ETHEL MANNIN

Ethel Mannin and a copy of her Connemara Journal.

Socialist writer Ethel Mannin spent three solitary months in a three-room cottage in Connemara. Thereafter the famous author cum travel writer wrote about her experience in her book *Connemara Journal*. The well-thumbed copy I have tells me it cost ten shillings and sixpence. It's a wonderful recollection of time spent sheltering from Atlantic gales and incessant rain and afterwards admiring the quality of the light in the land and seascapes. The 'silence so deep you find yourself listening to it'.

I'll let Ethel Mannin herself give you a taste of Connemara in the middle of the 20th century through her lamplight reflections on life, death, books and people. She wrote this just after the Second World War in 1946: 'It has been a bitter grey day of icy gales, and by evening the rain is splattering against the windows. At midday the turf man came with his shaggy pony and his orange-wheeled cart, Throwing a cartload of turf into a shed is not a thing to do in an icy wind; it is not only that one's hands and feet get frozen, but that the wind blows the fibre-dust from the turf into one's eyes. But a shed full of turf is a good, comforting sight… 'Out here, in these half dozen cottages dumped down amongst the great bare boulders as old as time, no one bothers with a radio – I don't myself – and a newspaper is merely something you buy if you happen to be going into town; and there is no cinema in the town, and none for miles, and only a morning and evening bus into Galway, and it is fifty miles away. Out here there is time enough, time enough to stand and stare. To lean upon a wall and listen to the wild, lost cry of curlews, and the sobbing call of a donkey, or the clatter of a cart along the boreen, for all such sounds are part of the deep peace of the bog and mountains and water – and men and women living out their lives in the calm acceptance that there is no hurry, and therefore no worry, because there is, blessedly, time enough ...'

Ethel Mannin, who died aged 84 just before Christmas in 1984, was one of Britain's most popular novelists and travel writers. The fact that she was born into a family with an Irish background shines through many of her books and articles. Dubbed an anarchist by some, she initially supported the Labour Party but became disillusioned in the 1930s. Initially sympathetic to the Soviet Union, a 1936 visit there left her disillusioned with Stalinism, which she described in her book South to Samarkand. According to the Irish historian and academic Dr Roy Foster, she was a member of the Independent Labour Party, and her ideology in the 1930s tended to anarcho-syndicalism rather than hard-line Communism, but she was emphatically and vociferously left-wing.

Clifden on a soft day in the 'Seventies. *Picture by Bill Heaney*

Mannin's 1944 book *Bread and Roses*: *A Utopian Survey and Blue-Print* has been described by historian Robert Graham as setting forth 'an ecological vision in opposition to the prevailing and destructive industrial organization of society'.

In her seventies, Mannin still described herself as an anti-monarchist, republican and a Tolstoyan anarchist. She is said to have been involved in an intense but problematic intellectual, emotional and physical relationship with W B Yeats and also had a well-publicised affair with Bertrand Russell, the Ban the Bomb campaigner. It is remarkable that there was a touch of the Delia Smiths about her in that Mannin was not just a good cook but a passionate football fan who was the long-time chairwoman of Shrewsbury Town F.C.

Ethel Mannin's Connemara Journal was published in London
in 1946 by John Westhouse. Price 10s and 6p.

Back in the day – fishing boats in the harbour at Roundstone, Connemara.
Picture by Bill Heaney

Chapter 11
CONNEMARA COOKBOOK

Marian Feeney at Ocean View, Sellerna, Cleggan, and whiskey cake.

Marian Feeney, who owns the Ocean Wave B&B and guesthouse with her Connemara fisherman husband Mike, rolls out the red carpet for visitors. She also does an excellent full Irish breakfast in her house overlooking the ocean at Sellerna, west of Cleggan. This is a peaceful and welcoming Connemara farmhouse, owned by a family who have a long tradition of fishing and farming. You will find a sign there with a warm Irish welcome that quotes W.B. Yeats: 'There are no strangers here, only friends you haven't yet met'. Ocean Wave, as its name suggests, is situated on the edge of Cleggan Bay, surrounded by sandy beaches, breath-taking views of the islands and mountains. Marian's husband, Mike' and friends go mackerel fishing in his currach from the tiny pier down the road at Rosadillisk. If you are lucky you might be around for a fish or two for the pan from his catch when he comes ashore. There are a number of really good guesthouses in Cleggan and Claddaghduff where you can lay your weary head after a day's walking in some of the freshest air in Ireland or swimming in the perfectly clean blue sea. Some of the women – and men - of these houses, where they all serve superb, old fashioned, full Irish breakfasts, have come up with recipes for favourite Connemara dishes. Be assured though, you will find the best of food and hospitality no matter where you choose to stay. And by the way the breakfasts are so delicious that even if you do have a 'a head on you' the morning after a night singing in Sweeney's Strand Bar or Oliver's or Richie Newman's or seeing the head off foamy pints in the Pier Bar, or wherever, you will manage to eat it. It will set you up for the day. Josephine DeCourcey, who owns Hazelwood farmhouse with her husband, PJ, said: 'All the guesthouse owners get along well together. We look upon ourselves as a team on a mission to provide the best possible food and comfortable rooms for our guests, who do us the honour of coming to stay with us here in Connemara.'

Marian Feeney's Irish Whiskey Cake

Make one 23 x 13cm/9 x 5in cake

Ingredients

175g/6oz of chopped walnuts
75g/3oz raisins
75g/3oz currants
115g/4oz plain flour
5ml/1 tsp baking powder
1.5ml 1 ¼ tsp salt
115g/4oz butter
225g/8oz caster sugar
3 eggs, separated
5ml/1 tsp grated nutmeg
2.5ml/1 ½ tsp ground cinnamon
85ml/5 tbsp Irish whiskey

Method

Preheat the oven to 160®C/325®F. Base line and grease the loaf tin. Mix the nuts and dried fruit with 30ml/2 tbsp of the flour and set aside. Sift together the remaining flour, baking powder and salt. Cream the butter and sugar until light and fluffy. Beat in the eggs yolks. Mix the nutmeg, cinnamon and whiskey. Fold into the butter mixture, alternating with the flour mixture. Beat the egg whites until stiff. Fold into the whiskey mixture until just blended. Fold in the walnut mixture. Fill the loaf tin and bake until skewer inserted in the centre comes out clean, about 1 hour. Cool in the tin.

The Ocean Wave,
Cleggan,
Co. Galway
Tel: +353 (0)95 44775
Email: oceanwavefeeney@yahoo.com
Website: www.oceanwave-bedandbreakfast.com

Josephine DeCourcey's Seafood Pie

Josephine DeCourcey looks after guests from Lucerne in Switzerland at Hazelwood in Cleggan.

Ingredients
600 grams potatoes
100 grams butter
50ml cream
50 ml full milk
Salt to season

Method
Cook potatoes and drain well
Place milk cream and butter in saucepan and bring to boil
Pour over potatoes while mashing

Ingredients
150 grams salmon cut in cubes
100 grams haddock
10 large prawns
150 grams cod
70 grams already cooked
50 grams butter
50 grams flour
50 ml cream
150 ml fish stock
100 grams leeks sliced fine
250grams parsley
30 ml white wine
50 grams shallots
50 grams cheese sliced thinly

Method

Place butter into a thick based saucepan and allow to melt, add shallots and cook gently add flour and cook into a roux. Add the stock to the roux and whisk to form a sauce allow cook while stirring with a wooden spoon to thicken. Add cream and white wine. Add the fish and the leeks allow simmering until fish is nearly cooked. Place seafood into pie dish, pipe potatoes on top and cover with cheese cook until golden brown.

Hazelbrook Farmhouse Connemara
Cleggan, Clifden, Connemara, Ireland
Telephone / Fax 353 (0)95 44646
E-mail: decourceyhazelbrook@eircom.net

Bernie Hughes Irish Soda Bread

Bernie Hughes in the kitchen at Cois na Mara and Irish soda bread.

Ingredients

250g plain white flour
250g plain wholemeal flour
100g porridge oats
1 tsp bicarbonate of soda, one 1 tsp salt
25g butter and 500ml of buttermilk

Method

Preheat the oven to 200C/gas 6/fan 180C and dust a baking sheet with flour. Mix the dry ingredients in a large bowl, then rub in the butter. Pour in the buttermilk and mix it in quickly with a table knife, then bring the dough together very lightly with your fingertips (handle it very, very gently). Now shape it into a flat, round loaf measuring 20cm/8in in diameter.
Put the loaf on the baking sheet and score a deep cross in the top. (Traditionally, this lets the fairies out, but it also helps the bread to cook through.) Bake for 30-35 minutes until the bottom of the loaf sounds hollow when tapped. If it isn't ready after this time, turn it upside down on the baking sheet and bake for a few minutes more. Transfer to a wire rack, cover with a clean tea towel (this keeps the crust nice and soft) and leave to cool. To serve, break into quarters, then break or cut each quarter in half to make 8 wedges or slices – or simply slice across. Eat very fresh.

Cois na Mara B&B
Cleggan
+353 (0)95 44647
coisnamara@hotmail.com

Noreen Higgins' Connemara Chowder

Noreen serving up her fish dishes at Oliver's in Cleggan, Connemara.
Chowder serves 6

Ingredients

7 ozs of salt port
3 large onions, coarsely chopped
6 small potatoes, peeled and diced
2.25 lbs of haddock or cod fillets
2 tblspns of flour
1.5 pints of milk
3 teaspoons of dried thyme
Salt and pepper to taste

Method

Remove any rind from the salt pork and discard. Dice the pork and fry in a large saucepan until golden. Remove and reserve the pork which should be dried kitchen paper. Then brown the onions in the pork fat. Boil the potatoes in a casserole dish for 5 minutes in just enough water to cover them. Cut the fish into small pieces (about one inch square) and add them to the casserole. Remove the onions from the pork fat and sprinkle them over the fish and potatoes. Discard any fat remaining in the pan and sprinkle the flour into it before stirring in the milk, thyme, salt and pepper. Pour the contents of the pan into the casserole and cover before leaving to simmer over a low heat for one and a half hours without stirring. Check the seasoning is to your taste and sprinkle with the pork you have reserved just before serving.

Oliver's on Cleggan Pier
Cleggan Fishing Village
Connemara
Co. Galway, Ireland
++353(0)9544640
oliverscleggan@gmail.com

Mary King's Apple Tart

Mary King of Cnoc Breac provides excellent amenities and food for visitors.

Ingredients

200 g shortcrust pastry.
3 medium cooking apples.
Sugar (to sweeten).
Egg to glaze.
Method
Make pastry
200 g plain flour.
1/4 teaspoon salt.
100 g fat (lard or margarine)
Cold water. (about three tablespoons)
Sieve flour and salt into a bowl.
Cut fat into flour with knife, then rub with fingertips, until mixture looks like fine breadcrumbs. Add water very little at a time, and mix with a knife to a smooth stiff dough. Turn onto a slightly floured board and knead lightly until smooth. Chill in refrigerator. Grease large oven-proof plate. Divide pastry in two, roll out each half and place one half on plate. Peel, core and slice apples. Place apples on pastry on the plate. Sprinkle the sugar on the apples. Brush edge of pastry with water and cover with second round of pastry, pressing edges well together. Cut a slit in the centre to allow steam to escape. Brush with beaten egg, place in a hot oven, 230 centigrade, 450 Fahrenheit, Gas 8 for 10 minutes. Reduce to a moderate oven for 25 minutes. Serve with whipped cream or custard.

Tom and Mary King
Cnoc Breac
Cleggan
Connemara
Telephone: +353 (0)95 44688
http://www.cnocbreac.com/

Loretta O'Malley's oysters

Loretta O'Malley of Harbour House at Cleggan Pier
preparing oysters for her guests at
Harbour House, Cleggan. Phone: 353 (0)95 44702
harbour.house@oceanfree.net

Oysters are a speciality at Harbour House, which has magnificent views of Cleggan Bay and overlooks the busy pier, where you can catch the ferry for Inishbofin. Old oyster hands insist that they're best eaten raw, perhaps with freshly ground black pepper and a squeeze of lemon juice or drop of Tabasco sauce. However they can be steamed, grilled or poached, too, and they make excellent canapés. Oysters can be battered into tempura, simmered into a sauce to serve with robust flavours such as beef or pork or even cooked with cream and served inside a hollowed out brioche roll.

Eileen Mulkerrin's barmbrack

Eileen Mulkerrin welcomes guests at Sea View,
Knockbrack, Cleggan, Connemara. Phone: +353 (0)95 44679
https://www.bedandbreakfast.eu/bed-and-breakfast/cleggan/sea-view-b-b/151696/

This recipe makes a lovely, moist loaf, which oozes flavour from the riche mixed spices and dried fruit, which have been left overnight in cold tea and Irish whiskey to soak up all the goodness.

Ingredients

375 g (13oz) packet of mixed dried fruit
50 ml (2fl oz) of Jameson whiskey
250 ml (9fl oz) cold tea
butter, for greasing
225 g (8oz) plain flour
2 tsp baking powder
125 g (4½oz) soft light brown sugar
1/2 tsp mixed spice
1 large egg

Method

Collect the mixed dried fruit in a bowl and pour over the whiskey and cold tea. Allow the mixture to soak up the liquid overnight. Pre-heat the oven to 170°C (325°F/Gas 3). Grease and line a 900g (2lb) loaf tin. Combine the flour, baking powder, sugar and mixed spice in a bowl. Make a well and break in the egg, then use a wooden spoon to mix it with the dry ingredients. Add a drop of the liquid from the mixed fruit and mix it through. You want to achieve a wet dough. Stir in the mixed fruit until everything is thoroughly combined. Spoon the wet dough into the lined loaf tin, place on the middle shelf in the oven and bake for one hour. Remove from the oven and allow to rest before removing from the loaf tin and placing on a wire rack. Cover in cling film and foil and allow to sit for a couple of days before serving it with some good Irish butter and a nice cup of tea or coffee.

Frenchwoman Odile le Dorvan at Kermor,
Streamstown Bay, Claddaghduff
Phone: 353 (0) 95 44698. kermor@eircom.net

We should point out immediately that this is NOT Odile's recipe. We wouldn't want to get her into trouble with the law. It is for Poitin Cake. Poitin (pronounced putcheen) is an illegal drink which was made by moonshiners back in the old days in Connemara. Illegal stills were concealed high up on mountainsides and in hedgerows in remote, low lying fields. They could also be discovered occasionally by prying Gardaí eyes amid rocks or in caves on the seashore. Secrecy was one of the main ingredients – the others were barley and potatoes - of this powerful alcoholic concoction. It is a clear spirit which looks like vodka or Bacardi rum. Simply take Marion Feeney's recipe for Irish Whiskey Cake (at the beginning of this chapter) or Eileen Mulkerrin's barmbrack recipe and replace the whiskey there with poitin. Not that you will find any around Cleggan or Claddaghduff, of course. It has however come into some people's possession in mysterious circumstances. Visitors have been known to discover bottles of poitin in a variety of strange places. They thought it was holy water. At least that is what they told the Customs Officers at the airport when they were going home.

Riders to the sea – horse lovers riding from Cleggan to the strand between Claddaghduff and Omey Island in Connemara. *Picture by Bill Heaney*

Clockwise: Fruit or the full Irish breakfast, Connemara ponies; Currach at Rosadillisk; A music session in Mannion's pub in Clifden; Horse riding at Claddaghduff strand and French guests enjoy their breakfast at Kermor, Streamstown. *Pictures by Bill Heaney*

Chapter 12
THE BIG WIND

Spectacular sea on the run as the Wild West wind gets up at Aughrusmore.
Picture by Heather Greer

The Wild West Wind

By Grainne Fricker

We have all heard of the Wild West Wind, but I had never really experienced it until this winter in Cleggan. I was trying to carry an electric heater around the corner of the Coastguard Station, which sits on the brow of a hill high above the village, only to find that it acted as a sail. Both the heater and I took off and were deposited a few yards away, upsetting Anna Conroy's neatly-stacked turf. Having got back inside the house I found that there was no way I could open the door against that wind in order to get back out again. It was bad enough being housebound, waging a futile battle with the elements and with a growing feeling of apprehension about the stability of the glass door; bad enough until the first slate went, and then the second, third and fourth and on into apparent infinity. Little by little everyday activities became disrupted. The wind howled down the chimney and scattered ash from the turf fire all over the house. What had, up to then, been the business of coping easily with a refreshing morning shower became an athletic feat of dodging cold rain which poured

with ever-increasing volume through a hole in the ceiling. I determined to forsake hygiene for a day or two until the storm had abated. But it did not.
If anything it got worse. By Monday it had got down to its destructive work with a vengeance. The Irish Lights ship glittered in Cleggan Bay. The sea heaved and tossed the boats as they sought shelter. Watching them from the safety of the back window in Oliver's pub they suddenly took on a vulnerability that I had never noticed before. The stories about such storms told by the fishermen became almost tangible.
One of the greatest pleasures Cleggan has to offer is the beauty of its walks. Even in weather of this ferocity, one simply has to get out, if only to do a little shopping. This simple exercise reduced Anna and me to having to cling to each other and any available wall to make it out to the car. One thing I did learn from this storm is that a Renault 4 is not constructed to cope with gale force winds. Driving in general took on a new aspect as nervous drivers avoiding flying slates broke into sudden bursts of speed, especially when passing the more dangerous houses. People took to parking in new 'safe' places around the village.
My own first comments that the storm was 'interesting and exciting' drew looks of gentle contempt around the bar. But as I listened to the growing inventory of damage to people's houses, I wondered at their patience in giving me an audience at all. Peter Walsh nodded his head in his own inimitable way. 'It's bad,' said Peter. And if Peter said it was bad it was bad and no two ways about it.
There was no more talk in the pub about bullocks and the price of hay. Nothing only the price of slates and windows and the ongoing cold, the wind and the rain, everyone with shoulders hunched over a pint simply waiting for the storm to end.
What struck me more than anything during that week was the spirit of the people of Cleggan, their unswerving loyalty to one another and their willingness to give a helping hand wherever it was needed?
As for myself, living in a house with slates or no slates, I was delighted to have an excuse to extend my holiday and stay on for an extra few days. Who could travel to Dublin in weather like that?

Wonderful walks down colourful roads like this one at Emlough and Rosadillisk. *Picture by Heather Greer.*

Iris at Emlough pictured by *Heather Greer*.

Cleggan

A place of beauty
Where each word spoken
Takes me back and down
To the mushy roots
Of the wild burning iris.
Thick broad blades
Hugging sap
Invaded by greenfly froth
Even the dung smell
Becomes potent:
Heady bog cotton
Tripping above darkness
No one thing
Remains inert or silent.
Each breath tugs
With inexorable, unqualified power
Rising like the evening light:
A silken cloth
Ripping over Sellerna

Grainne Fricker

The circus comes to Connemara

Jugglers practising in Merrion Square, Dublin.
Picture by Bill Heaney

The crowd cheered and clapped as the famous juggler walked out with several small balls in his hands. Then, as the atmosphere changed, the tent was filled with silence as he climbed up the ladder to the wire. An assistant tied a blindfold around his eyes and he started to walk across the wire juggling at the same time. Nobody clapped as they knew it would only distract him and he might fall. When he reached the end of the wire the applause that rose from the crowd was something you would be really proud of. Next came two shiny-nosed clowns. The children's faces lit up with excitement as their favourite heroes appeared in an old car that was supposed to be going from Donegal to Dublin. The car, as you can well imagine, kept breaking down. Each time this happened a clown gave it a kick. Then all of a sudden the clowns and the car disappeared. Next came a fire-eater who ate the flames as if he was eating potatoes. He had eyes like coals of fire and great big muscles. But the star of the night was Mighty Dave himself. He lifted a donkey and a Shetland pony over his head as we all looked on in amazement. All too soon the last act was over. I will not forget for a long time all the fun we had when the circus came to Cleggan.

Nicola O'Toole (then aged 12).

Connemara Clock

Connemara clock

For many months I lay in the window of a small shop overlooking a busy street. People passed by, up the street and down the street. Some would stop occasionally and press their noses against the window pane to have a look at the other things in the window. Nobody ever looked at me. I always felt so sad. Then one day and old lady came along and said to the shopkeeper: 'How much for that clock in the window?' He replied: 'Ten pounds.' The old lady said she would take me. I was brought to an old house and put on the mantelpiece. I knew that I would not be happy there. I was never dusted or polished and I stopped frequently. The old lady was not satisfied with me and one day she brought me back to the shop where I was bought. The shopkeeper was not happy to see me coming. He put me back in his window. One cold winter day a little girl called Niamh came along. She was staring at me for a long time. Then she said to the shopkeeper: 'I would like to buy the clock in the window.' The shopkeeper put me in a nice little box and gave me to Niamh.

I have been in Niamh's house for many years now. Each day Niamh winds me and dusts me and occasionally I am polished. But I work for Niamh too. Every morning I ring my alarm to waken her in time for school. Even though I am getting old now I still have a good time.

Niamh Laffey

Claddaghduff and Omey Strand

St Feichin's Church on Omey island off Claddaghduff.
Picture by Heather Greer

The name Claddaghduff translated into English means 'the black shore'. It is in this village in the parish of Omey and Ballindoon that I have been living since I was born. Claddaghduff overlooks Omey Strand and the island of Omey itself. Beyond that there is the great Atlantic Ocean. This is a place of great scenic beauty. Omey beach is a very safe place for children. There is a pool in the middle of the strand which never dries out and in it many children learn how to swim. When the tide is out you can walk across the strand to Omey Island where there are big sand dunes. On the island as well there is an old church which was excavated from the dunes some years ago. It is known as St Feichin's Church and every year on the saint's feast day in January, Mass is celebrated there. When my grandfather was a young man there were very few houses in Claddaghduff, but that has changed and now there are lots of new houses. Claddaghduff hall used to be the school and was known as Aughrus School. The church in Claddaghduff is one of the most beautiful in this part of Ireland and children from the primary school sing there at Mass. Claddaghduff is a very nice and interesting place to live. I would not like to live in any other place.

Caitriona King

Riders from Cleggan enjoy cantering with their horses on Omey Strand.

Barefoot in the sand at Omey Island in Connemara. *Pictures by Bill Heaney*

Chapter 13
MICHAEL LONGLEY

Poet Michael Longley – inspired by scenes like this in colourful Connemara.

It was a hitch-hiking holiday around Connemara, South Mayo and the Aran Islands with his wife Edna and fellow poet Derek Mahon that turned out to be a prelude to hundreds of visits to the West of Ireland by Michael Longley, *writes Bill Heaney*. In this first volume of *The Poet's Chair*, Longley – whose poetry has transcended political and cultural boundaries throughout his career – reflects on what has influenced his craft. Belfast-born Longley opens with an 'autobiography in poetry' where he recounts the poets and poems and places that have influenced him as both a reader and writer of poetry. And Connemara, Westport, Leenane, Louisburgh and Inishmore feature large amongst the many places he has visited and written about. Longley says life in Belfast was demanding and painful in the 'Sixties because one of his friends was having a breakdown. He writes: 'We were drawn perhaps to the idea of the place, Connemara.'

Longley quotes Tim Robinson, the Roundstone-based writer and map maker: 'Connemara – the name drifts across the mind like cloud shadows on a mountainside, or expands and fades like circles on a lake after a trout has risen.' That other Belfast poet, Louis MacNeice, whose family have clerical connections with Clifden and Omey Island, is quoted too by Longley. MacNeice wrote: 'The very name Connemara seemed too rich for any ordinary place. It appeared to be a country of windswept open spaces and mountains blazing with whins and seas that were never quiet.'

Longley recalls in this odyssey around the West: 'In Galway we boarded the steamer for Inishmore – a very rough crossing – there were no stabilizers on the boat – below decks Mahon and I fought off sea sickness with medicinal brandies. In Kilronan we hired a jaunting car that took us to our guest house.'

Longley says it rained most of the time and that he huddled in an attic bedroom in a sleeping bag, chain-smoking. But the turbulent weather and the fact that he could not speak Irish didn't put him off from getting around the island. He writes: 'Between showers we walked around the rocky fields in flashing, soul-irradiating light. Our brief sojourn would become

part of my inner mythology. We felt sad leaving the island.'
His response was to write 'Leaving Inishmore' which was the first of his West-inspired poems to survive.

It includes the lines:
Miles from the brimming enclave of the bay
I hear again the Atlantic voices

Longley and Mahon returned to Aran a year later, in 1966, at Easter. He writes: 'On Good Friday, Derek and I were very moved when we witnessed the islanders, in their best tweeds, walking on their knees over the stone flags into the church. It is striking that my first collection (of poems) and the first collections of Derek Mahon and Seamus Heaney all contain poems about the Aran Islands.'

Seamus Heaney, Longley and other poets have travelled on the ferry to Inishbofin.
Pictures by Bill Heaney

In this excellent volume of prose and poems, Longley goes on to discuss his close relationships with Mahon and Heaney, who has written about Inishbofin, Maam Cross and Recess, as well as other poets from around the world. It is a very personal discussion about how the West of Ireland has had a deep impact on his poetry, his life, and his 'spiritual education'. Longley's love of nature and the environment shines through and the extracts from his poems portray his deep understanding of the West. *One Wide Expanse* gives readers a rare insight into the creative process of one of Ireland's leading contemporary poets who was Ireland Professor of Poetry from 2007 to 2010.

Michael Longley was educated in Belfast and went on to study Classics at Trinity College, Dublin. His most recent collection *The Stairwell* (2014) won this year's Griffin Poetry Award. He is married to Edna Longley, a critic of modern poetry, and they have three children. The Ireland Chair of Poetry has, since 1998, been a key element in the promotion, discussion and encouragement of poetry – both its practitioners and readers – across the island of Ireland. John Montague, Nuala Ní Dhomhnaill, Paul Durcan, Michael Longley, Harry Clifton have all held the role of Ireland Professor of Poetry for three years each, with Paula Meehan, the current Professor until 2016.

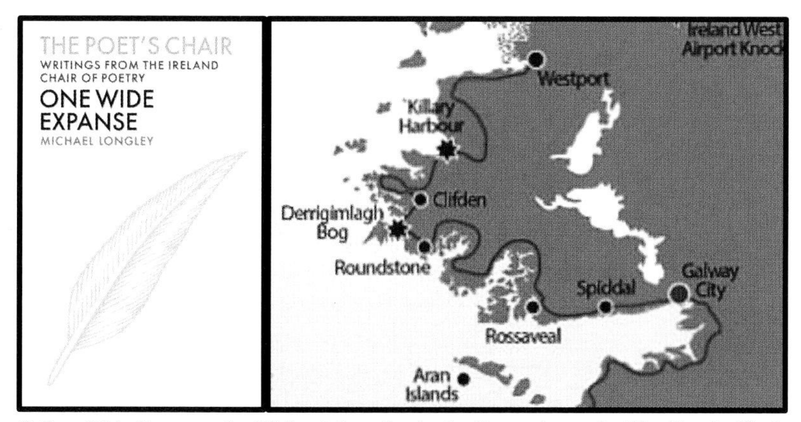

**** One Wide Expanse by Michael Longley is the first volume in The Poet's Chair series from UCD Press, which has now published the public lectures of each of the three most recent Ireland Professors of Poetry.***

Chapter 14
TOMMY WHELAN

The Black and Tan prison guard watching seems bewildered at the calmness of the two men Paddy Moran (left) and Tommy Whelan waiting their execution.

Events surrounding the execution of *The Forgotten Ten*, who include Tommy Whelan from Clifden in Connemara, are touched on in a new book which examines 'unknown or neglected aspects of the Irish Revolution,' *writes Bill Heaney.* Twenty-one-year-old Whelan was one of a group of men hanged in Mountjoy Prison during the troubled period from 1920-1921. Volunteer Thomas Whelan's death and its aftermath, which led to two RIC police officers being gunned down in the street in Clifden, and half the town being burned down in an act of revenge, is frequently recalled in the capital of Connemara, even now in the 21st century.

Journalist Padraig Yeates's new book ***A City in Turmoil*** makes reference to these tragic events as he tells how ordinary people came to terms with life when ambushes were a daily occurrence and civilians were increasingly caught in the deadly crossfire. And how crowds of many thousands – there were 40,000 outside Mountjoy the day Thomas Whelan went to the gallows – had to endure the pain and suffering of their countrymen being executed.

All this was happening on top of other impositions including restrictions on travel, military curfews and the threat of internment constantly hanging over them.
The main thrust of Yeates's book, which is a follow-up to his ***A City in Wartime: Dublin 1914- 1918,*** concentrates on the role of the Bank of Ireland in keeping Dublin Corporation solvent and preventing the city coming to a standstill. Yeates records the rise of the municipal reform association to challenge the dominance of Sinn Fein and Labour. He recounts the events surrounding the execution of Volunteers Thomas Whelan and Patrick Moran, of Crossna, Roscommon, on March 14, 1921, the beginning of St Patrick's Week. And how the events of 'Bloody Sunday' in 1920 were the catalyst for the executions and the Black and Tan outrages that followed.
It all kicked off in Dublin early on the Sunday morning, November 21, with when Michael Collins' deadly plan to wipe out the so-called Cairo Gang was clinically implemented.
IRA teams shot dead 13 people and wounded six others. One IRA member, Frank Teeling, was captured, but he escaped. The audacity and efficiency of the IRA operation terrified and crippled British intelligence in Ireland and caused other informers to flee into hiding. Believing that the assassins had concealed themselves in the crowds heading for Croke Park that afternoon, a force of Black and Tans drove there in Crossley tenders. Dublin was playing Tipperary, before a crowd of 5,000 spectators, and it was their intention to search everyone in the stadium - but frustrations were at breaking point. Without warning, the soldiers indiscriminately opened fire on the players and into the crowd and, in the mayhem that followed, 14 people were killed and more than 60 wounded.
In her book***, Beyond the Twelve Pins - A History of Clifden and District 1860 - 1923,*** Connacht historian Kathleen Villiers-Tuthill chronicles how the British authorities were as appalled at this atrocity as were the people of Dublin. In an effort to calm the situation, Dublin Castle issued a statement claiming the Black and Tans were fired on first by gunmen in the crowds. This was totally dismissed as a pathetic cover up, however, and ***The Times***, a pro-Unionist publication, ridiculed the Castle's version of events. A Labour Party delegation in Dublin at the time totally rejected the Castle's view and Brigadier Frank Crozier resigned in protest at the attempt by the authorities to condone the unjustified actions of the Black and Tans.
Suspects who were rounded up included 21-year-old Tommy Whelan, the sixth child of 13 children, whose parents owned a small farm on the Sky Road in Clifden. Whelan was arrested on November 23, 1920, and, on February 1 of the following year, he was charged with the death by shooting of Captain G.T. Baggelly, an army prosecutor. He told the court martial he was innocent. The prosecution cast doubt on the reliability of the eyewitnesses for Whelan, arguing that as Catholics they were not neutral. The defence complained that it was unfair to suggest the witnesses 'were prepared to come up and perjure themselves on behalf of the prisoner', because 'they belonged to a certain class and might hold certain political opinions'.
The court, however, trusted the evidence of an Army officer who lived in the same house as Baggelly and who had identified Whelan as the man covering him with a revolver during the raid. There was also testimony by a soldier who had passed by the

house when he heard shots fired and who said he saw Whelan outside, attempting to start his motorcycle.

Tommy Whelan's mother pictured in Dublin outside the gates of Mountjoy Prison, where her son was executed.

Whelan, despite his protests of innocence, was found guilty of murder and sentenced to death. He was hanged at 6am along with Patrick Moran, the first of six men to be executed that day.

Padraig Yeates's book states the crowds outside the prison were even bigger than those at Kevin Barry's execution. Dramatic details of what happened inside the prison before the executions were given to the press by the clergy, who said both Whelan and Moran had served Mass in the chapel at 5am. Whelan is said to have sung during the Mass and when it came time for communion a Black and Tan, Lester Collins, who had guarded the condemned men knelt beside them at the altar rails to receive the Eucharist. A report in the ***Irish Independent*** stated: 'Both men walked firmly and fearlessly to the scaffold, where final words of comfort and consolation were uttered by the attendant chaplains.'

Tommy Whelan's unfortunate mother, who had kept a vigil at Mountjoy from the time her son was incarcerated, sat on a chair outside the prison gate, wrapped in her Connemara shawl against the morning cold. The trip to Dublin was her first experience on a train and she was allowed visit her son as many times as she wanted. She said he was treating being sent to his death in the manner of a man getting ready to attend a football match.

In the days leading up to the executions, people gathered outside Mountjoy eager for news of the prisoners. Mrs Whelan became a favourite with everyone. Dublin's Lord Mayor inquired if she was comfortable in her lodgings, and looked after her. On the eve of his execution Tommy is said to have told his mother and visiting friends that he was happy and' was perfectly prepared to meet his death with a clear conscience. The

night before he died, Tommy Whelan said he would sing the old traditional Connacht song: 'The Shawl of Galway Grey' – and he did.
At 8.25am next day, a notice was put on the prison gate saying that all executions had been carried out according to the law. There was despair in the crowd. As execution followed execution, the Labour Party and the two rival trades councils in Dublin called a half-day strike in protest at the hangings and no trams, trains or ferries ran that day. Shops and public houses closed as a mark of respect for Patrick Moran, who was an ardent trade unionist and was president of the barmen's and shop assistants' union. Two days later the IRA followed through with their threat of reprisals. RIC constables Charles Reynolds and Thomas Sweeney were shot dead in revenge for Whelan's death at E.J. King's Corner in Clifden. This was the beginning of Clifden's nightmare torching by the troops.

City in Turmoil by Padraig Yeates is published by Gill & Macmillan in Dublin. Clifden Main Street, which was the scene of the shootings of the RIC men.

Chapter 15
HISTORY WALKS

Historian Kathleen Villiers-Tuthill recounts the history of Clifden.
Pictures by Bill Heaney

Nothing pleases like nostalgia, history and knowing your roots. People, old and young, queued up in the Market Square to follow historian Kathleen Villiers-Tuthill up steep Church Hill to Clifden's Christ Church. They were keen to explore the graveyard where the Connemara town's history is written in stone – on the gravestones of the deceased. And they could have no better guide than Mrs Villiers-Tuthill, who has written at least six books about the town, including *Colony of Strangers*, published by Connemara Girl Publications.

The event was part of the Clifden Community Arts Festival and Christ Church workers were on hand to supply tea and coffee and host a popular plant sale by the local gardening club. Mrs Villiers-Tuthill gave a large group of visitors and local people a wonderful insight into how the town was founded by John D'Arcy in 1812. She told of the community's joys and sorrows, episodes bad and good - and how various characters connected with it had built it up into the successful town it is today. The meeting place for these tours is now at the Station House Hotel in Clifden.

Visitors and local people gathered in Christ Church graveyard to hear Kathleen Villiers-Tuthill's talk on how Clifden was born and the colourful background of the people who have lived there.

Know your Irish inside out and upside down

Bill Heaney visits the statue of Padraig O'Conaire in Galway.

If you love Ireland and the Irish language you will love this book. Connemara man Brian Ó Conchubhair has selected five stories in this bilingual collection, which give a glimpse of the genre's trajectory from the beginning of the last century to the early years of this one. The poet Pádraic Ó Conaire, whose statue stands in Galway's Eyre Square, opens the collection, followed by Máirtín Ó Cadhain. Both will be well known to speakers of Irish, O'Conaire especially because of his famous *M'asal Beag Dubh, My Wee Black Donkey.* Happily, the other authors – Pádraic Breathnach, Joe Steve Ó Neachtain and Micheál Ó Conghaile – are all still with us. All five pieces are excellent. If you are not fluent in Irish you can read the evocative translations concerning life, love and loss with pleasure. If you are fluent you can reacquaint yourself with original writing and be the better for it. To read in one language or the other, one must turn the book upside down. That way you are bound to know your Irish inside out.

Lost in Connemara: stories from the Irish edited by Brian Ó Conchubhair and published by Cló Iar-Chonnacht is available on-line and in good bookshops. Guideline Price: €12

Clifden Main Street in the 1950s.

Chapter 16

SAINTS AND SOCCER STARS

Head in the clouds – St Patrick's mountain, Croagh Patrick, from the Quay in Westport, Co Mayo. *Picture by Bill Heaney*

Saints, including St Patrick himself, saw Connemara as a stopping off point on the road while seeking out lonely coves and tiny islands on which to establish monasteries. Here in the back of the back of beyond in the 5th century you will find the beginnings of the Land of Saints and Scholars. A book by the retired Church of Ireland Archdeacon Anthony Previté, *A Guide to Connemara's Early Christian Sites* is brimming with information for travellers seeking to discover the pilgrim paths of the western seaboard. The Clifden clergyman spent years scrambling around the sometimes inaccessible offshore islands, and remote headlines along the Connemara coast. He describes 25 early monastic sites which illustrate that Christianity had a foothold in Ireland even before Patrick arrived on the island. Some notable Irish saints are associated with Connemara including Patrick who, on his way to Croagh Patrick in Co Mayo, rested on a bed, drank water from a well, and wrestled with the devil at Maum Eán in the Maam Turk Mountains.

Other saints have left evidence of their presence and there are the remains of a little chapel or oratory dedicated to St Ciarán on the hill An Bhinn Bhuí, at Kilkieran (Cill Chiaráin), the small fishing village six miles east of Carna in Irish-speaking South Connemara. St Ciarán, who studied under St Enda on Inishmór on the Aran Islands, founded the famous monastery on the Shannon at Clonmacnoise, renowned for centuries as the great centre of Irish learning. St Brendan the Navigator, whose sea exploits were recorded in a famous book *Navigatio Brendani*, and whose monastery at Clonfert became one of Ireland's great schools, is associated with a graveyard on Omey Island (Ollabrendán). Brendan also bequeathed a holy well and monument of Inishnee Island across the bay from the wonderfully scenic Roundstone village. And St Columcille is reputed to have founded a monastery at An Bhánrach Bhán, near the eastern entrance to Cashla Bay. Columcille is credited with having established no fewer than 100 Christian settlements, including those at Derry, Durrow, and Kells and most famously at Iona in the Outer Hebrides of Scotland. The remains of St Leo's oratory are found on Inishshark (Inis Airc), whose last 23 inhabitants were evacuated from the island in 1960. St Keelan (St Caolánn) wrote a life of St Brigid and built a church on Croaghnakeela Island (Cruach na Caoile), two miles north west of St MacDara's Island. St Féichín, a popular local name, built a fine stone church which was totally covered with sand until an excavation uncovered it on Omey in 1981.

On High Island, subject of an eponymous poem by Richard Murphy, there is evidence of another foundation by St Féichín. The island is also associated with St Gormgal, and there are the remains of a monastic settlement.
Picture by Bill Heaney

There are various Holy Wells at Renvyle, Cleggan Head, Aillebrack, Doon Hill and Mweenish Island and many ruins of religious foundations. St Mac Dara's island, whose distinctive stone church was repaired in the 1970s, is one of Ireland's most famous Christian monuments. Mac Dara was a favourite with fishermen and even today boats passing his island still dip their sails in a gesture of respect. On High Island, subject of an eponymous poem by Richard Murphy, who lived for a time at Cleggan, there is evidence of another foundation by St Féichín. The island is also associated with St Gormgal and there are the remains of a monastic settlement, including a chapel, dwelling cells, a water mill, enclosure walls, graves, numerous stone crosses and a reservoir and pond.

These early Christian missionaries and hermits were tough, according to Archdeacon Previté, who expresses admiration for them for having stood up to the wild weather on these storm-blown and isolated settlements. Yet, he writes that they obviously had tremendous skills as stonemasons, metalworkers, farmers, mariners and artists. Together with their writing of manuscripts, copying of the Gospels, and their religious and daily disciplines these are testimony to their hardiness, skills, and their ability to survive.

Station Mass in a Connemara cottage is a painting by Aloysius O'Kelly and hangs in the Irish National Gallery in Merrion Square, Dublin.

Meanwhile, a valuable impressionist painting that had been considered lost for more than a century turned up in priest's front room in a chapel house in Scotland. The 19th century work by leading Irish artist Aloysius O'Kelly is thought to be worth around £600,000. It is considered so significant that the work was sent for display at the National Gallery of Ireland in Dublin. The painting, entitled *Mass in a Connemara Cabin*, had been on the wall in a presbytery of St Patrick's church in Edinburgh. It went on public display for the first time in over a century at a Mass in the church in 2002. It was cleaned in 1990, but nobody recognised it as the missing work or realised its significance. The truth came to light when Father Richard Reid, a Redemptorist priest at St Patrick's in the Cowgate, started researching the artist on the internet. He said: 'I typed O'Kelly's name into the internet not expecting anything, and I discovered this painting had been missing for 100 years. Then I got into a panic. The painting was authenticated but it will not be sold, despite the fact that the church needs money for refurbishment. This painting is more a part of Irish than Scottish history. But it belongs to the people of this parish and that is one of the reasons for not selling it.'

The painting was exhibited in the Paris Salon in 1884 as the first painting of an Irish subject to be shown there. The artist emigrated to the United States in 1895 after which the painting disappeared from public view. It may have come to St Patrick's during the 1890s through the then parish priest Canon Edward Hannan, who supported Michel Davitt and the Irish land reform movement. The artist's brother James was a Westminster MP and agitator for land reform and many regard the painting as clearly political. It depicts a priest celebrating a Station Mass during penal times when Catholicism was ruthlessly suppressed in Ireland. Look closely at it and you will see his top hat on a chair near the makeshift altar, which is the kitchen table. The parish of St Patrick's, part of the Diocese of St Andrews and Edinburgh, has given the painting to the National Gallery of Ireland in Dublin on long term loan.

Pat Ward, whose father came from Aughrusbeg, and Jim Mulkerrin in Scotland and Accrington Stanley shirts, whose father was born on Omey Island.
Pictures by courtesy of Agnes Mulkerrin

Parish priest Canon Hannan was one of the founders of Hibernian Football Club in Edinburgh. The Cowgate area where the church was situated had become known locally as 'Little Ireland' due to the large number of Irish immigrants living in the area. Canon Hannan's uncle was Monsignor Richard B. O'Brien, who founded the Catholic Young Men's Society (CYMS) in Ireland in 1849. One of the parishioners of St Patrick's was James Connolly, who led the 1916 Rising in Dublin. Young men, who took to playing and watching football at the Meadows, a public space at the heart of the capital, were rejected from signing on with clubs due to the fact that they were Irish Catholics. At this time there was a much anti-Irish feeling in Edinburgh. At the foundation of Hibernian, Canon Hannan was elected Life President of the football club. Membership was exclusively for members of the CYMS and meetings were held in the Catholic Institute. Failure to attend Mass meant exclusion from playing. Hibernian – like Glasgow Celtic, which was formed in 1888 by Brother Walfrid from Ballymote, Co Sligo - was set up as a charitable institution and over the years carried out some wonderful work for the poor people irrespective of their religion. When the club applied to join the Edinburgh Football Association, they were informed that they must first apply to Scottish Football

Association, who in turn informed the club that they only catered for Scotsmen and that Irish were not permitted. In 1876, Hibernian Football Club were finally admitted to the Edinburgh FA and, after playing at numerous venues, land was acquired for the first Hibernian Park, which was situated where Bothwell Street in Edinburgh now stands. Its home ground today is in Easter Road.

There is a Connemara connection with Hibernian in that people who played for them included Pat Ward, who also wore the blue of Leicester City. Pat was the son of John Ward from Aughrusbeg and my own aunt, Charlotte Heaney, from Dumbarton. Charlotte was Mary Ward King's best friend. Jim Mulkerrin, who was a top goal scorer, played for Hibs, Accrington Stanley and Scotland and has to this day relatives who live on the rocky shore road behind the chapel in Claddaghduff. Jim's father was born on Omey Island before the family were evacuated to the landward side of the causeway there. The Connemara link with Hibernian continued with Stephen Woods, son of John, becoming their goalkeeper. Stephen is now the Celtic goalkeeping coach. Peter Goldie, who also played for Celtic, and visited Connemara is the husband of the late Emma Ward, sister of Pat.

A Guide to Connemara's Early Christian Sites is published by Oldchapel Press and is beautifully illustrated. It costs €15.

Items you might find a typical Connemara cottage in the Irish National Folk Museum at Castlebar in Co Mayo. *Picture by Bill Heaney*

Chapter 17
COMFORT IN CONNEMARA

The Station House Hotel in Clifden, capital of Connemara.

The privations of yesteryear do not apply to the Connemara of today where, if the weather is unkind – as it can often be – there are wonderful places to shelter. In Clifden, the capital of Connemara, there is comfortable accommodation available at the Station House Hotel – the comedian Billy Connolly's grandfather was a porter at the railway station there – or the Foyle's Hotel, the Alcock and Brown or the Abbeyglen Castle Hotel on the way out the Sky Road. There are any number of excellent bed and breakfast places and guesthouses from Clifden to Cleggan to Claddaghduff. The people are warm and friendly and you can toast your toes at a turf fire in the welcoming hotels and public houses and enjoy a pint of foaming Guinness or a golden glass of hot Irish whiskey. If you want a change from dinner in a hotel there are a myriad of restaurants in Clifden's two main streets - Main Street and Market Street - where you can enjoy freshly caught fish and shellfish, beef or lamb and vegetables from the kitchen garden. A nice crab salad or a smoked salmon sandwich, accompanied by freshly-baked soda bread and a glass of wine in the comfort of the Marconi Restaurant or E J King's public house, are always available.

Way to go – a cyclist takes a breather near St Joseph's Church in Clifden.
Picture by Bill Heaney

Walking, cycling and horse riding are favourite with visitors to Clifden and you can take the scenic Sky Road and travel on from there to the villages of Claddaghduff and Cleggan, where again you can enjoy the freshest of fresh seafood at Oliver's or a welcome pint in Joyce's, Newman's or the Pier Bar. In Cleggan, you can stay overnight at Josephine DeCourcey's Hazelbrook farmhouse – there is a huge choice of B&Bs - and in the morning catch the red ferry boat skippered by Pat Concannon to Inishbofin. This is an island paradise for cyclists, walkers, bird watchers and wild flower enthusiasts. There you can hire a bike and pedal along at a leisurely pace over the quietest of roads through scenery and seascapes that will take your breath away. And what could be nicer than to put your feet up with a good book from The Clifden Bookshop, where Nicole and Maire are ever helpful with advice?

The Signal Bar at the Station House Hotel in Clifden, Connemara.

Chapter 18
BOLTHOLE FOR A POET

Peaceful place for a poet to put down roots, Doonreagan in Connemara.

Think of the poet Ted Hughes, and what images come to mind? The English countryside and its wildlife, perhaps, ***writes Arminta Wallace of the Irish Times***. The death from suicide of his wife Sylvia Plath, almost certainly. What probably won't flash into your head is a picture of the wild and wonderful coastline of Connemara. The Yorkshire-born poet had a substantial Connemara connection, and it's the subject of a short play, *Doonreagan,* which was staged at the Station House Theatre in Clifden. Three years after Plath's death, Hughes and his new partner, Assia Wevill, rented a house near Cashel, Co Galway, with their three children. The plan was to build a new life together, far from the expectations – and condemnations – of the London literary scene. Hughes's response to the open spaces of Connemara was ecstatic. It was at Doonreagan that he began work on his epic series *Crow: From the Life and Songs of the Crow*, the first poetry he had written following Plath's death. For Daniel Simpson, who created the role of Hughes in London and now reprised it for an Irish tour, the landscape plays a central role in the drama.

'There were all kinds of complicating factors and pressures going on in his life,' says the actor. 'Not least the persecution that he was suffering from the ever-strengthening feminist movement at the time. They blamed him for Sylvia's suicide. After an extraordinary period of writer's block, he more or less fled, really; not just to Ireland, but to Connemara, and then to Doonreagan within Connemara. As a Yorkshireman, the natural world was so important to him when he was growing up and fed into just about everything he did in terms of his work. And I think the natural world, being so raw here, just allowed him to reconnect and emerge again.'

Wevill, a city girl of Middle Eastern origins who had built a successful career in the advertising business, wasn't so sure. 'It's awfully unsheltered,' her character says of the house early in the play; a reaction that will strike a chord with anybody who has attempted to unpack a picnic on a windy day in the West. The beauty and tranquillity of Cashel Bay eventually won her around. But there was to be no happy ending for Wevill, played in this production by Tara Breathnach. Three years after the events depicted in Doonreagan, Wevill would take her own life, exactly as Plath had done. And unlike Plath, who went to extraordinary lengths to protect her children, Wevill also killed her daughter Shura.

For author and director Ann Henning Jocelyn, the tragedies that swirl at the centre of this story come very close to home. With her husband, the 10th earl of Roden, the Swedish author and playwright is the owner of Doonreagan House. When Jocelyn discovered, quite by chance, that the poet had rented the property in the 1960s, she began to read everything she could find about the little-known interlude in Hughes's tempestuous life. Doonreagan isn't particularly kind to Hughes, a notorious womaniser who had left Plath to live with Wevill. Within a year of Wevill's death he was married again, to a nurse 20 years his junior; and there were many affairs along the way. Such behaviour makes Hughes easy to dislike. Still, after an in-depth study of the poet's life and work, Simpson is reluctant to condemn the poet out of hand.

The Yorkshire-born poet Ted Hughes, who came to live in Connemara.
Picture by Slideshare

He said: 'There's no shying away from the fact that women played a hugely important part in Ted's life. He needed women, and he made sure that women were always available to him. For whatever reason, that was a big part of who he was. You often hear examples of great creative figures who have quite troubled domestic lives or private lives – something just has to give. Ted was a huge and complex character.'

'After Sylvia died, Ted came in for this great collective condemnation,' he says. 'But what people didn't realise was that Sylvia had made a number of attempts on her life. Way before she even met Ted, she had these terrible mental health problems that unfortunately ran in her family. So it's just too easy, too neat to say that Ted had this extramarital affair and that caused her suicide. With Assia's death, it's much more difficult because Ted never spoke about what happened. So to get at the truth of what he felt about it is really tricky. We can never quite know what goes on within people's private lives, though we can get some sense of it from what both of them wrote at the time, and that's what the play explores. Their time in Connemara was one of their happiest periods, and Ted was desperate to stay.' Hughes hoped to buy Doonreagan when the lease expired. But the house was sold suddenly, and he and Wevill had to return to London. 'He really wanted to settle in Ireland,' Simpson says. 'So if circumstances had been different they would have stayed. And history would have been very, very different for them both.'

Clifden and the kind of scenery that attracted poets such as Ted Hughes.

Chapter 19
CONNEMARA CULTURE

Sheila Pratschke, chair of the Irish Arts Council.
Pictures by Bill Heaney

Clifden is 'a shining example' of how the Arts must be rooted in community - and serve that community, Sheila Pratschke, chair of the Irish Arts Council, told a large audience when she opened the Clifden Arts Festival in Connemara. Ms Pratschke said she was honoured to perform similar functions around Ireland – 'It is always an opportunity to thank people for their hard work and to reiterate a message close to my heart – we are all in this together, artists, art organisers, the Arts Council and so many generous sponsors, bringing art to the public whose right to a rich and meaningful cultural life we are here to serve.' She added however that Clifden was 'a bit special' – and posed the question 'where else could one find such a rich and varied mix of traditional, contemporary and classical music, comedy and theatre, prose and poetry, visual Arts and family fun?'

The *An Chomhairle Ealaion* chair explained: 'When we say in the Arts Council that the Arts must be rooted in community, must serve community, we can always point to Clifden as a shining example of how this works and how this matters. The particular emphasis this Festival has always placed on involving local schools and young people, on encouraging them to discover their own creativity as well as that of others, has been one of signal accomplishments.' She said the Arts Council, which is the national development and investment agency for the Arts, should be adequately resourced. Ms Pratschke added there would be no limit to the Council's imaginative ambition for art, artists and audiences in Ireland – 'We are a proud country and a proud people. We have a rich and valuable sense of ourselves and of each other. The spirit of the *meithal* is not dead here. We still remember that we live by and for and with each other. We are proud of our poets and singers, our painters and dancers, musicians, actors, playwrights and novelists – and we are equally proud of our communities, our children, our neighbours and our friends who give so generously of themselves so that life may be richer for us all, more meaningful, more enjoyable, more dignified and more significant.' The Arts Council has published a strategy outlining the guiding principles by which they intend to work over the coming decade, which entails the provision of public funding which would see the Arts practised and enjoyed widely in communities and public spaces. Ms Pratschke said: 'We see an Ireland where local and national politicians, decision makers and officials in a wide range of departments and agencies recognise and acknowledge the distinctive societal values of the Arts and provide for them accordingly.' If someone asked her what do the Arts really mean to you in Ireland, she would reply: 'I could do no better than hand them a map and point them West. Go to Clifden I would say, go to Clifden while the Festival is on and see for yourself.'

Enjoying the opening event of the Festival are Moycullen artist Padraic Reaney and director Brendan Flynn. *Picture by Bill Heaney*

Meanwhile, Moycullen artist Padraic Reaney exhibited his Crazy Jane portfolio in the West Connemara Leisure to mark the 150th anniversary of the poet William Butler Yeats. Clifden Arts Festival artistic director Brendan Flynn said Padraic's work was an inspiration which was greatly appreciated when it was put on show at the Galway Arts Festival in 2003. People were queueing up to view Padraic's paintings in Clifden. He said Crazy Jane was WB Yeats's alter ego, the person who acted outrageously as he himself would like to have done had he not had his public reputation to protect. For example Yeats writes of her after she has had a tumultuous row with a shopkeeper as having stomped off to the pub and drank herself into 'a state of drunkenness of epic proportions'.

Poet Paul Durcan signs his new collection of poems for Sheila Pratschke, chair of the Arts Council/An Chomhairle Ealaion at Clifden Arts Festival.

Mr Flynn, one of the founders of the Clifden Arts Festival, joined Chairman Des Lally and Secretary Kathleen Mannion in thanking everyone involved in the participation, organisation and sponsorship of the events. The award-winning West Coast Grupai Cheoils and Ceili Bands and Clifden Comhaltas provided the opening night entertainment. These young performers and musicians were led by their teacher, Marie Walsh, in a lively arrangement of traditional Irish music, song and dance. Meanwhile, the pre-opening entertainment was provided by True North, a C&W band who have been coming to the Clifden Festival annually for 13 years. The audience was treated to a new Connemara song written by True North's lead singer, Dennis (Dusty) Walsh, *Clifden by the Sea.* The band flew in from the US for the Clifden gig and Dusty said: 'I have always been inspired by Clifden and that's what made me write this song. I hope local people like it.'

Tenor Finbar Wright gave a splendid performance to a packed house in St Joseph's Church during Clifden Arts Festival.

Leading personalities from the world of music and literature appeared at the Festival including tenor Finbar Wright, Brendan Sheen, celebrating 50 years in show business, poet Paul Durcan and novelist Mary Costello plus the great Christy Moore. There were also children's events, art exhibitions and guided walks around the historic town of Clifden. Derry's Phil Coulter was scheduled to be there in 2016. The economic impact of Clifden Arts Festival on Connemara is a cash injection of 1.3 million euro, it was revealed at the official opening. Solicitor Nessa Joyce, president of the Clifden and Connemara Chamber of Commerce, said an average of 10,800 people attended Festival events. And visitors to the town generated 4,000 bed nights for hotels and guesthouses. Ms Joyce said: 'I would like say how fortunate we are to have such a wonderful Arts Festival here in Clifden for the last 38 years and the Chamber is delighted to be one of the sponsors of such a successful Festival.' She revealed that last year an Economic Impact Study was carried out evaluating the value the Festival brings to Clifden. And Nessa laid it on the line for the large audience with figures and percentages:

- The Festival attracts an audience of 10,800.
- 30% are locals
- 35% are domestic visitors
- 35% are overseas visitors
- People attend an average of 3.6 events = 3,012 attendees.
- 78% are in Clifden at this time because of the Festival.
- The average satisfaction score (max = 10) is 9.1.
- The economic impact of the Festival is €1.3 million.
- The Festival helps to support the equivalent of 40 jobs.
- The Festival generates just short of 4,000 bed nights.
- 75% of businesses say that Clifden Arts Festival increases sales.

She added: 'I am informed that ticket sales are well up with a growing interest from both national and international visitors which means more business in town.'
Ms Joyce congratulated Brendan Flynn and his hard working team of volunteers who run the Festival and all those who participate in it. She said: 'Every year it goes from strength to

strength and it always delivers an exceptional and inspirational programme of cultural activities that encompasses literature, poetry, art, theatre, film and diverse musical events. No sooner has one Festival finished than plans are underway in preparation for the next year's programme. Not only is the Festival so important to the business community it is also important for all the community and especially the school children who from the age of four years of age have access to such a range of 'The Arts' that come here to Clifden from all over the world for these 10 days.' The Festival Finale had a Mardi Gras atmosphere with as wonderful parade, fireworks amazing aerial acrobats. Nessa said: 'Clifden, for a small town, really punches above its weight.' One of the most popular events of Clifden Arts Festival was the reading given by the Mayo poet Paul Durcan in a packed Clifden Station House theatre. Durcan's moods swing from comedy to tragedy and embrace harrowing intimacy, politics and love. Many of his poems are set in the remote West of Ireland. This has made the great man himself one of Ireland's best known and best loved writers of poetry. Paul Durcan's readings from his latest collection *The Days of Surprise* enthralled and entertained the large Connemara audience and there were queues for more than an hour afterwards for signed copies of book which is published by Random House.

The lovely and hugely talented Elizabeth Cooney on violin and classical pianist Finghin Collins. *Picture by Bill Heaney*

Class as in classical

Classical music has always played a major part in the Clifden Arts Festival, *writes Bill Heaney*. The festival enjoys a reputation for quality rather than quantity in this field of music, however. The appreciative audience at Christ Church in the Connemara town were treated to just that – classical delivered with class. Violinist Elizabeth Cooney and pianist Finghin Collins gave a wonderful performance of works by Schubert, Symanowski and Elgar. Elizabeth proved she is one of the most talented violinists in Ireland and Finghin is quickly building an international reputation for himself. This duo turned Christ Church into a cathedral of music, making the most heavenly sounds imaginable. The event was sponsored by Helen and Vincent Foley, who must be congratulated for helping to bring such wonderful music west of Galway city.

Gilbert and Sullivan come to Clifden

Fun and laughter at the brilliant Gilbert and Sullivan's Trial by Jury in the packed Clifden Courthouse during Festival Week. *Pictures by Bill Heaney*

From the top - The award-winning West Coast Grupai Cheoils and Ceili Bands and Clifden Comhaltas provided the opening night entertainment. Solicitor Nessa Joyce. After the storm – a beautiful morning in Clifden. Novelist Mary Costello with Nicole Shanahan, of the Clifden Bookshop. *Pictures by Bill Heaney*

Chapter 20
TRADITIONAL MUSIC

Mairtin O'Connor and Cathal Hayden at Clifden Arts Festival.
Picture by Bill Heaney

Music was at the heart of the Clifden Arts Festival – but there was lots of comedy too. Best joke of the Festival came from accomplished Oughterard-based accordion player Mairtin O'Connor:

Q: Did you hear what happened to the guy who couldn't afford the payments for the exorcist he employed to cast out his devils?

A: He's been repossessed!

That post banking crash and mortgage crisis joke was not the only reason the audience in Clifden's Station House Hotel theatre had to smile. The quality of the traditional music produced by Mairtin, Seamus O'Dowd and Cathal Hayden brought great pleasure to a large, appreciative crowd of music lovers. Mairtin is a magician on the accordion and almost made it talk; Seamie was a sensation on the guitar and a fabulous singer, and Cathal topped it off with a faultless performance on the fiddle and banjo. Co Galway man Mairtin is one of the most respected and best loved musicians ever to emerge from Ireland and was one of the main musical forces behind the legendary Riverdance phenomenon. He has taken all his experience with bands De Dannan, Midnight Well and Skylark into The Mairtin O'Connor Trio where his ground-breaking expertise on the accordion is astonishing. Cathal's also a top man who played with Four Men and a Dog, and Seamie O'Dowd's abilities have become increasingly familiar at international Festivals. Hotelier John Sweeney and his wife Treena, who sponsored the event, were delighted. 'They're brilliant – the best technically at the traditional stuff that I have ever seen,' said a Californian woman, who has taken up residence in Cleggan. 'In America, the droughts meant my land dried up and I was running out of water to keep my horses. So I decided to sell out to the government and come to Connemara where there's plenty of both – Connemara ponies and water, plenty of water.'

Another group of musicians, who are still in embryo and waiting to be born into a tight knit band, are Kathleen Macinnes, Dermot Byrne, Brian Finnegan and Mike Vass. Kathleen, from South Uist in the Hebrides, sang as Gailge and is a natural performer with a wonderful, soft lilt in her voice. She has appeared previously at the mega popular Celtic Connections festival in Glasgow. Accordionist Dermot Byrne is one of those quiet guys who concentrates deeply and knows how to knock a fine tune out of a squeeze-box. Armagh flautist Brian Finnegan is without doubt one of the finest whistle and flute players this side of the Atlantic. Guitar player and vocalist Mike Vass, from Nairn in the Scottish Highlands, has been described by an American music writer as 'sublimely beautiful and lyrical'. A quiet, under-stated guy, Mike is also an accomplished songwriter.

Kathleen Macinnes, Dermot Byrne, Brian Finnegan and Mike Vass. Kathleen, from South Uist in the Hebrides, sang as Gailge. *Picture by Bill Heaney*

Meanwhile, Jackie Daly, Matt Cranitch and Conal O'Grada turned on the traditional music style at the Clifden Arts Festival. The men from Sliabh Luachra in Co Kerry brought a special guest with them from their own part of the country, Bernard O'Donoghue, the Oxford poet. It was an interesting mix, which greatly pleased the packed audience at the Clifden Station House Hotel theatre. The music was brilliant and the poems were fantastic. 'I thoroughly enjoyed the experience,' said Bernard. 'It's the first time we have had a poet up here apart from meself,' joked the inimitable accordionist Jackie Daly to his fellow musicians, Matt on the fiddle and flautist, Conal.

Clockwise: Jackie Daly, Matt Cranitch, Bernard O'Donoghue and Conal O'Grada. *Pictures by Bill Heaney*

Chapter 21
FAIR DAY FOR POETS

Donegal poet Moya Cannon – a breath of fresh air at the Clifden Arts Festival.
Pictures by Bill Heaney

It's like a Fair Day for writers and poets and musicians and we all love it, Donegal poet Moya Cannon told the Clifden Arts Festival in Connemara. 'There's a terrific bustle about Clifden and it gives us all a chance to meet up here,' she said. Moya, who was born in Dunfanaghy, brought a large following of friends, fans and family from Donegal, Galway and Dublin with her to the Clifden Station House Hotel theatre for the launch of her latest collection of poems, *Keats Lives.* And a wonderful book of poems it is, infused with 'our visceral attachment to the beauty of the earth, with music, with language itself and with archaeology'. There's even a poem about daily life as we know it here in Ireland – Classic Hair Design.

It's the tale of an old lady with great determination to keep going in life at the age of 92, and whose weekly visit to the hairdresser for the same cut and set she's been having for years since she married. 'It's a signal to the world out there that she's definitely not finished with life just yet,' said the poet.

One of her poems, *In the Textile Museum*, ends:

Love slips easily through the eye of a needle,
Words clothe us;
Not everything ends up in a book …

Moya was introduced to the large Clifden Station House audience by Roundstone-based Tim Robinson, writer and cartographer of note on all things Connemara and the Aran Islands. Her readings were interspersed by some beautiful harp playing by her good friend, Kathleen Loughnane and writer-in-residence Tony Curtis presented Moya with a bouquet of flowers.

- *Keats Lives by Moya Cannon is published by Carcanet Press and is available from all good bookshops and on-line.*

Film promotes relationships between Irish and Scots

Meanwhile, Festival-goers in Clifden were treated to a showing of a new film about promoting relations between the Scots and Irish. Young Irish film maker Donal O'Ceilleachair's movie – *From Cchuil Aodha Go hOilean I – From Coolea to Iona* – made its Connemara debut in the Station House Hotel cinema. It is centred around a journey made from Ireland to the Hebrides by Cor Chuil Aodha – the Coolea Men's Choir. They were accompanied by President Michael D Higgins and Scottish Government ministers Fiona Hyslop and Mike Russell. The choir occupies a special place in Irish music and embodies the spirit of area that is historically rich in both poetry and traditional music.

It was founded by composer Sean O'Riada in 1963 and continued after his death in 1971 by his son, Peadar. The intimate documentary follows the life of the choir over an eight-week period, charting its weekly trials and tribulations under Peadar's watchful direction. The visit to Iona, which includes takes from the boat trip from Oban to Mull, was made to mark the choir's 50th anniversary. This is the third film in Donal O'Ceilleachair's Irish Music Trilogy. Galway poet Moya Cannon also launched the DVD of the highly acclaimed *Dreamtime Revisited* about the late, great Connemara man, John Moriarty, whose memorial lecture was delivered this year by Father Peter McVerry SJ. Newry-born Peter was ordained in 1975 and since that time has devoted his life to helping homeless young people in inner city Dublin, campaigning vigorously for them.

At the Gaelic film debut in the Station House Hotel theatre – Josephine Quinlan, Brendan Flynn, Donal O'Ceilleachair, Moya Cannon, poet Michael Coady and Lynn Hill, neighbour and friend of John Moriarty from Horse Glen, Toombeola, Connemara. *Picture by Bill Heaney*

Chapter 22
SONG THE SOLDIERS SANG

Novelist Jennifer Johnston was one of the star guests at Clifden Arts Week.
Pictures by Bill Heaney

She is without question one of Ireland's greatest living writers. Jennifer Johnston's novels have been published across the world to great acclaim. And now she has graced the Clifden Arts Week in Connemara with her presence and a reading in the Station House Hotel theatre. It wasn't just a reading however – it was a very special reading, a world exclusive in fact, a scoop for her fans, friends and festival-goers. For Jennifer read to a large audience the first chapter of her new novel, which had still to be published. She indicated that she was unhappy with her publisher's decision to keep *Naming the Stars* under wraps – and not to have it on sale in the bookshops for Christmas. Just out of hospital, where she spent eight weeks recovering from a hip operation, Johnston was patently frail of body but strong in spirit and voice. Walking with the aid of a cane, she sat in an armchair to give her warmly received talk, which stimulated lots of questions about how she went about her work. One question she refused to answer however the name of her favourite amongst her own books – 'That's a bit like asking me which one of my children I like best.'

Poet Michael Coady, who welcomed Johnston, said: 'Jennifer is constant and consistent and is one of the great pillars of Irish literature.' Johnston said the fact that the novel would not be published at that time 'annoys me intensely', but it was something she would have to live with. *Naming the Stars* is about the way families react to the news of one of their own being killed in conflict. It's about the way people mourn and how Johnston's principal characters, Flora and

her daughter, cope after their father is killed in the desert at the Battle of El Alamein in Egypt. And how they are haunted and confused by the singing of the German song *Lili Marleen* in German by Marlene Dietrich – 'All the soldiers sang it at night in the desert to take their minds off what might happen to them the next day.' Johnston, who writes prolifically, produced *Captains and the Kings*, and *How Many Miles to Babylon* in the Seventies to *Sixpenny Song* in 2013. This event was sponsored by writer and cartographer Tim and Mairead Robinson, of Roundstone. Jennifer Johnston was awarded a Lifetime Achievement Award at the Irish Book Awards in 2013 and is a member of Aosdana. East Galway novelist Mary Costello was delighted to be in Connemara for the Clifden Arts Festival. Mary told the audience in the Station House Hotel theatre that she's been away too long. And that in the time it took driving out the N59 from Galway she saw not one, not two or three but four rainbows between the sunshine and showers - 'I just had to get out of my car and take photographs with my phone.'
Connemara is obviously a place Mary has loved since childhood – and still loves very much. In her debut novel, *Academy Street*, Costello describes a pretend marriage – it is sealed by jumping over broomsticks and having a sheepdog as the celebrant - between Tess, the story's principal character, and an elderly, kindly farm labourer, whom she adores. In that part of the novel, they go off to live happily ever after in Connemara. That is the dream however. The actuality is far different. Life is not a children's game. Tess's mother dies from tuberculosis when she is just seven years old. The little girl is shocked to the extent that she is left literally speechless. Words return to her lips however when she accidentally bumps into something on the farm and lets out a shout. That is when the joyous pretend marriage takes place in celebration of her voice returning. Tess is brought up by her sisters and an irascible, angry father who is desolate at the death of his wife, which has left him bitter. He makes life more than difficult for his children who naturally drift away from the big country house, a house similar to one where Costello's mother was brought up, near the town of Mountbellew. It is a house with a history dating back to the Famine when it was utilised as a hospital to accommodate more than 400 patients, around half of whom died. They were buried in the grounds of the house Costello calls Easterfield, in ditches and fields, in a quarry and under trees.

This is a haunting, spell-binding story which eventually switches from the slow pace of East Galway life to busy, bustling New York, where Tess becomes a nurse, living in a small flat and following in the footsteps of her late mother. Costello, whose reading in Clifden was one of the highlights of a very successful Arts Week, says her book was never intended to be 'an emigration novel'. It has turned out that way however and, in my view, it is up there in that genre in quality with Colm Toibin's *Brooklyn,* which has been made into a successful film.

Costello's book was launched in Dublin and was short-listed that same day for the prestigious Bord Gais Energy Books Awards. It has received tremendous praise from other young novelists of note, including John Boyne, and Maggie O'Farrell, who said: 'I read this book from cover to cover in one night.' This is a beautifully written and researched story about a young Irish woman who bravely faces the twists and turns of a life of great beauty and would have been forgotten had this novel not been written. It is full of happiness, hazard and heart-break over a period of the latter half of the 20th century. Nobel laureate Andre Brink is unstinting in his praise for Costello's work – 'It is not just graceful but heart-breakingly so …'

Academy Street by Mary Costello is published by Canongate, Edinburgh

East Galway novelist Mary Costello has produced a stunning debut novel.

Chapter 23
WALTER MACKEN

Walter Macken, whose stories are set in Connemara.
Picture by Jimmy Walsh

One of the saddest things about the death of Walter Macken at the comparatively young age of 51 is that the Galway writer had ideas for books, plays and story lines that would have kept him busy for another ten years at least. Galway's internationally famous bookseller Tom Kenny revealed this in a hugely interesting talk on Macken's life and work at the Clifden Arts Festival, which has become an unmissable event on the Irish culture calendar each September. Galway-born Macken wrote the first historical novels about Ireland and based many of his best-selling books and plays on his beloved Connemara, including *Rain on the Wind*, the bookseller's own favourite novel. Macken was always 'Wally' to Tom since they were young men and the author cum actor courted his sister, Peggy, who became news editor of the *Connacht Tribune*.

'The other name doesn't sound quite right and Wally's what we all called him from whenever I knew him,' Tom revealed in the Clifden Station House theatre, where he had the audience hooked from the point where he said Macken and Peggy had eloped to Dublin after his father intervened because he wasn't well enough set up for his sister. She had established herself in journalism in a prestigious post and Macken was on the very lowest rung of the ladder in *An Taibhdhearc* in Middle Street. This was where they met when Peggy, joined the theatre company and attended her first rehearsal. It was evident to those listening that they were about to hear a family insider's version of the life of a great man. First, however, Tom told a 'possibly apocryphal' story about his father who was the editor of the *Connacht Tribune*. He heard this from a police sergeant's son in a pub in Roundstone, Connemara. The man said his policeman father had been first on the scene at the Alcock and Brown landing in Clifden and had taken the two men home to get cleaned up and have their dinner. The sergeant then rang the *Connacht Tribune* to say he had a story for the paper but before he was prepared to reveal his piece of news, a world exclusive, he wanted to 'discuss the percentages'.

Tom returned then to the Macken story and the eloped couple who had moved on to London where Macken worked as an insurance salesman, riding around the city on a bicycle collecting payments for a wage of just £7 a Festival. Eventually they moved back to Galway and lived at Menlo, which was close enough to the town and the Savoy cinema, one of Macken's favourite haunts. The author was an avid reader and wanted nothing more than to find a place to write in peace and quiet, but he had to have an income and so took up acting again at An Taibhdhearc, where he managed the place and did everything from selling tickets to painting the scenery. Tom said his brother-in-law was seen by some as 'a bit of a tyrant' but that was because 'he was always looking for perfection. He was a perfectionist.'

Tom Kenny delivered his talk on Walter Macken at the Clifden Arts Festival in Connemara. *Picture by Bill Heaney*

Some great actors were attracted to An Taibhdhearc, including Siobhan McKenna and Sean McClory, and audiences came from all around to see the productions there. However, the directors of An Taibhdhearc were not content and wanted only plays written in Irish staged there. Macken was unhappy since this would have meant repeat after repeat of the few Irish language plays there were and he had translations done of great plays by such as Sean O'Casey and Eugene O'Neil. 'That didn't suit the director though who continued to put pressure on Wally,' said Tom.

Macken was having some success with his writing and had his first novel, *Quench the Moon*, published by Macmillan, the publishing house owned by the family of the UK Prime Minister Harold Macmillan. It was an extraordinary novel set in Connemara and it was extremely successful,' said Tom, who added that Macmillan were delighted. So pleased were they in fact that Harold Macmillan gave an advance of £3,500 to Macken to buy a house in Glan, near Oughterard, that the writer had fallen in love with from the moment he first saw it. 'That was a vast sum of money at the time. 'He went home and told Peggy he had found just the place for them to live,' said Tom. 'When Peggy asked what it was like, how many rooms were there and what the kitchen was like, Wally said he didn't know. What he did know was that this was the ideal place, a dream of a place, where he could settle down and write.' The story of *Quench the Moon*, which was later banned by government censors, was about the ordinary people from Buttermilk Lane being moved out to the 'wilds of Shantalla'. The eponymous play went to the Abbey Theatre in Dublin and Macken went with it, but he tired of the repetition of productions, the same old flats scenery and sets and a lot of stage Irish stuff which he did not like. Meanwhile, his novel *Rain on the Wind* was winning awards and Macken was being lionised in the media worldwide and made offer after offer to appear on the stage, but there was only one thing he wanted to do which was write, write, write. The house at Glan was the place where he was able to do that and where visitors were warned not to disturb the great man, who went to Mass and Communion daily and spent a lot of time at his typewriter. Tom Kenny said that Macken took a long time to settle into the typewriter, and liked to have the stories composed in his head before he sat down to write. It was said that Peggy, his wife, wrote lots of his material, but that was patent nonsense, although her skills as a sub editor were of great assistance to him. She also helped to teach him shorthand and typing, skills which helped him to move material quicker, especially when his typing speed increased.

Macken was an occasional fisherman on the Corrib lakes, an inveterate smoker but not a drinker – 'I never saw Wally have more than one glass of wine.' He was an approachable man who spent a great deal of time speaking to local folk who would stop him in the street and wonder had he heard a particular story. They were hoping more than anything that they would see it in print in one of his books and that they would be identifiable and have that notoriety in the community. Macken would go out for long walks and sing little ditties, which had made up himself, along the way. He loved the Savoy cinema and used Kenny's bookshop as a kind of personal library. Tom Kenny said: 'He would take a book away and give us a verbal review when he returned it. That was very valuable to us in the business. It was great to know what was in vogue and what would sell.'

Macken wrote his famous historic trilogy in eight years – *Seek the Fair Land, The Silent People* and *The Scorching Wind* – while keeping himself going on magazine articles for the likes of the prestigious *New Yorker* magazine and other publications. He went back to the Abbey Theatre in Dublin for the 50th anniversary celebrations of the Easter Rising in 1966. Macken wrote a total of 17 novels and a host of plays, short stories and children's stories and set them locally in places like Inisbofin and Cleggan and along the Claddagh quays. He died however suddenly aged just 51 – 'It was very sad because that was really too young. The saddest thing about it was that he had the next ten years of his writing inside his head.' Tom Kenny said his brother-in-law, despite his fame, never had any high notions of himself and that he was a religious man who was deeply upset when three of his books were banned by government censors – 'The censorship in this country at that time was ridiculous. You had to be a really good writer to be banned. I would challenge anyone to go through all his work and come back to me and tell me they had found anything offensive. Wally had that great gift of common touch. He loved talking to people in the street. '*Rain on the Wind* is my own favourite book. I think you could say it was Galway's *Ulysses*. Wally Macken enriched my life and the lives of thousands of readers all over the world with his writing.'

Chapter 24
CHRISTMAS IN CONNEMARA

White Christmas – Connemara pony at Aughrus Lake with the snow-capped Twelve Bens in the background. *Picture by Heather Greer*

Christmas was tough in Connemara during the Emergency, which we called the Second World War here in Ireland. We were freezing cold having been down on the shore harvesting kelp for export to Scotland. These seaweed rods were used in the manufacture of iodine and alginates which are essential ingredients in the production of items like plastic, toothpaste and food in a factory near Girvan on the Ayrshire coast. Many of you will have seen it on the road from the new ferry port at Cairnryan on Loch Ryan, *writes Eoin King.* These war years were a hard time to be growing up on a tiny, boulder-strewn smallholding at the edge of the Atlantic. I would be about 16 and my brother John maybe 18 and there were people a helluva lot older than us working at the sea rods – and you got so numb and so wet that your hands and feet swelled with the cold and they got so cold and so numb you didn't feel the cold anymore. We also picked winkles or whelks. The worse the weather, the harder you worked because you needed the bad weather to rip the sea rods from the seabed and cast it ashore. Christmas and January were the same. You worked when you got the weed and you worked long hours in harsh conditions for very, very little. That would be from November until February in the depths of winter and the worst of weather. You harvested about six tonnes of wet matter for one tonne of dry matter and you sold that for £3. So, if you had ten tonnes of dry matter you got £30 for it. £30 would have a reasonable amount of purchasing power. At the end of the year you sold the complete crop. At Christmastime you didn't get anything – or have anything. You harvested the sea rods all through the winter and you collected them, you tied them when they were dry and you brought them out where they could be weighed. And in April you would sell the crop, and you would get a cheque for say £30 which would be the total value of your year's work.

I remember one Christmas when my brother John and I were working at the sea rods and we had absolutely nothing. How did we survive? My mother may have sold an animal or two through the year and she stretched the money for that out as long as she could and, well, you got a certain amount of credit from the shop. They knew that you were working, or not working, and your credit depended on that. My mother had got whatever groceries she could get from the shop – but that wasn't much, hardly anything at all. If my father was at home, which very often he wasn't because he was mentally ill and in hospital in Ballinasloe at that particular time, he would be getting about seven or eight shillings. And you would stretch it as far as you could. You would have sowed – you would have grown potatoes – and you would have straddled your neddy and you would have taken the potatoes to market and sold them in town. You put tackle like you'd see on a camel on your donkey and you hung on two panniers to the donkey and filled them with potatoes and you took them into town.

Now, to carry a load that distance you could not overload the animal, so the maximum load would be 14 stone, which would be 1 cwt and three quarters. It would be ten miles from Cleggan into Clifden where you would put your potatoes down in the marketplace and your potatoes would be bought. You would get sixpence a stone which would be seven shillings for 14 stone which today would be 35p. Now it's surprising what you could buy for 35p at that time.

White as an altar boy's surplice – snow on the Twelve Bens of Connemara.
Picture by Heather Greer.

A lone traveller in the storm at Aughrus; a Christmas robin, a redwing and a blue tit in the snow at Emlough near Rosadillisk. *Pictures by Heather Greer*

How cold were we? We were so cold we were frozen, and there was no special Christmas. There were several Christmases when you came home and what little you had was no more than you had at other times of the year. Remember at that particular time flour was very scarce. The only type of flour you would be able to get was just mixed wheat. You did not see any such thing as bacon or sausages and despite the fact that you were maybe due a ration of butter, but you could not even get the ration of butter. The staple diet at the time was dry brown crude bread made from crude milled wheat with no bran or pollard or anything extracted from it, or substitute coffee with milk you had produced yourself if you were lucky. You had no sugar most of the time and you got half an ounce of tea per person per week. But what would half an ounce of tea, little more than a tea bag. It was as little as that. Then you didn't get coffee at all. What you got was a substitute for coffee that tasted like anything but coffee, you got sugar; you got half a pound of sugar a week.

Eoin King working at the lobster farm at Aughrusmore, his cousin, John Woods, Mary Ward King, with her grandson, Michael Gordon, who is now resident in the US and the lobster ponds. *Pictures by Bill Heaney*

Everybody before the War had their own little village shop. Ours was Antoinette O'Malley's and we registered in that with our ration book. That was out the far side of Aughrusmore, beyond the monument on the hill there towards Claddaghduff. You had to walk there in every kind of weather and collect your rations. You got three and a half pounds of flour per person per week. You got half a pound of sugar and, at times, that went up to three quarters of a pound. You got half an ounce of tea. I don't know how much butter because whatever you were granted you never got it anyway.

There was no such thing as high days and holidays. They were all the same days. Mainly you had enough of potatoes. You would grow oats as well – there wasn't much of a market for it – and we grew wheat at times. We took it into town to Clifden and milled it. But you had eggs for part of the year, you had butter and milk – you had maybe an abundance of it – but come winter time when fodder got scarce the cows went dry and you just managed because there was no milk at all. You often drank tea without milk. You often drank tea without milk or sugar. Why people ever bothered with itself or coffee I have no idea. You would have been as well off drinking water.

My mother was left back at the house without anything. Sometimes we would eat potatoes twice in the one day. She had no leisure or recreation, no social life at all really, because she was too fully occupied patching clothes and drying clothes and mending socks and trying to get wool and knit socks and jerseys for us, to do the best she could to keep us dry and warm, which we never were. She always talked about her times in Dumbarton in Scotland, where she had come from, and she always cursed the day she ever left Dumbarton. The one thing I can say about her – and the one thing I appreciate about her, and this is true, she never showed emotion in so far as she never cried, she never complained. If she did, she did it in solitude. You would have to find her crying in the garden because she didn't want to discourage us. She could sing even though she was heartbroken. I don't know if she got a reasonable education in Scotland. All the same her sister, Maggie, was a teacher, who became a Carmelite nun, you know what I mean. Now the thing about it was if she got a chance of an education, I don't know if she ever did, she might have been a scholar. But she didn't. My mother's grandparents came from right in front of my place at Aughrusbeg. Her mother came from there and her father came from Inishbofin. Our grandparents lived back there then – Mary O'Sullivan was her name and Johnny Murray was his. Mary O'Sullivan was married to Johnny Murray, hence my mother's grandparents. And when all the family emigrated, my uncle Michael came back to stay with them (the grandparents). They emigrated to Scotland from here.
My grandfather came out of Inishbofin when he was just 12 years old. He stole a sheep because he had nothing. He sold the sheep for eight shillings and bought a pair of tackety boots and whatever clothes he had beside. He walked it to Sligo and he got the potato boat to Dumbarton, where he got a job on the Clyde, shipbuilding, where he lived and worked his whole life. His name was Michael Ward. He went to Dumbarton and he met my grandmother, who was Ellen Murray, and they got married there. Michael was the oldest child in the family, and as my mother's grandparents were getting older they were coming to see them and visit them and to try and help them and all that kind of thing. My mother too was coming and going from Dumbarton to look after her grandparents – she would be sent back to Connemara after they probably wrote to her father saying they were unwell and all that kind of thing and they had no one to look after them. So she came and she went, on and off.

Photo above is from 1956 and shows James Healy,(standing), and Mark Geoghegan, (on horse), pictured on the old Oughterard to Clifden Road.

The condition of the road here in 1956 indicates how remote and undeveloped Connemara still was even in the middle of the 20th century and a postcard from Clifden in the 1950s.

It was a different world at that time. For instance, you know the Imperial Hotel in Galway? She saw that with a thatched roof on it, my Mum did. And she came and went on the railway to Clifden, and the mail was brought from Clifden to Cleggan in a pony and trap, a jaunting car, a side car. She came to her grandparents' funeral. My Uncle Michael Ward – I don't know was it his grandmother or his grandfather it was died first, but which ever one it was he went to town to buy a coffin and when he got back with it the other one was dead and he had to go back again to get a coffin for the second one. That would all have to be done on a pony and sidecar. But my mother told me – now one of them died today, the other one died tomorrow – she heard her grandmother calling her – I don't know would they have telegrams at that time? And the word came through that she was dead. And so my mother was packed off to Ireland.
With her grandparents dead, she found herself living back at Aughrusbeg with her brother Michael, and my father was living in a house nearby with an aged father and mother. Michael announced he was going to go to America and there was a match to be made between my mother and Patrick King. It was a good arrangement, they said. If they married then they would get the two places – the two small farms - next door to each other and make them into one. She agreed and she went into the one house to look after Patrick King and his parents. I don't know how long she was in Ireland at that time. She never did admit that there was a match made. She always maintained it was a romance, but knowing my dad as I do, he was not the romantic type – not at all. I am nearly certain there was a match made at that time and I would hazard a guess that it was Michael Lacey's grandfather who made the match because he specialised in that kind of thing.
In Connemara we survived. I remember a time when the most you could get for a yearling or a year and a half, which say was 5cwts, would be £4. Well, you see that was quite a lot of money. I remember the big thing was with my mum or any other mother in her position that she would be able to provide a crude pair of boots for each of her children for going to school in the winter. In the summertime you went to school in your feet. You were never aware of your feet. But in the winter with the frost and snow you had better have protection. And I remember my mother going to town and she bought a pair of boots for me and I went down next door to an old man, Willie Davis, an ex-neighbour of ours, who made comment on my new boots. He asked what my mother had paid for them. I said 12 shillings. Oh, good Christ, he said, four shillings more than mine and he was an old grown man, you know what I mean. I got mine, he says, from Duggan's, Monaster House, Kilkenny Street, Dublin. You sent – you'd see it in the paper – eight bob, 40p, to get a pair of tackety boots by mail order.
Well, alright, if you sold an animal you got maybe £3 or £4. Now these animals were all set up to cover the winter to pay certain bills and all that kind of thing. It set you up for the winter. Now if the market was good then you might even have jobbers coming to the door to buy your cattle, but if the market was bad you might have to drive them into Clifden and offer them for sale on the Main Street and you might not even be asked what you wanted for them. Sometimes the jobbers would come along and they'd ask you, offer you a price which would only make one offer and that was what you got. Sometimes you might get a good price for them, but it was common for them to drive the price down as far as they could. They would come out on the road and offer you money and sometimes the price would change three or four times on the

way into Clifden. I did it myself, I walked them to Clifden. You did it with me one time, Billy, in pouring rain.

Everything was budgeted for at that time. You would probably have a bill you had to pay at the grocer's. You had to pay rates and rent and you had to – we don't have to pay rents and rates now. I'll tell you this; our land was bought by the Irish Land Commission in 1922. We were paying £28 a year to the landlord up until 1922. It was bought by the Irish Land Commission and it was divided up and given to us. You paid the rent to the ILC until you paid back the value of your portion of land. In 1962 it became ours, the land was ours. The Land Commission did well enough on it too because, you know what, our portion of land was valued at £32. Do you know what I mean? That would have been what the ILC paid for our land. That was £2.15s a year we paid from the time we got it from the Land Commission. We paid that twice a year by receivable order – in June and December. After a certain lapse of time you had the land paid with interest and I think you got a freehold after that. And back in 1972 the Fianna Fail government as an election gimmick abolished rates and we did not pay rates or interest from then unless of course you were a big farmer. I went to school the odd few days that I did go to a place right in Claddaghduff called Patches. It was a three teacher school originally with about 45 pupils going there. That was the whole school. One teacher taught infants and third class and she was the biggest anti-Christ on this earth and if she is in heaven today then I don't want to go there. When I left school my first job was chasing after the cows' tails at home. You waited for the school to end at 14 and you were out the school like greased lightning and you didn't give a tinker's curse that you'd starve. No, I did not get a job. I worked around the house sowing potatoes and cutting turf and doing the odd job for neighbours, drawing out turf from the bog for them and pulling in weed for them and drawing out manure for them and minding cattle. They paid you as little as they could manage which brought little or no comfort at Christmas in Connemara more than 75 years ago. *Eoin King was speaking to Bill Heaney.*

Rosadillisk Pier, where the fishermen left from on the night of the Cleggan Disaster.
Picture by Bill Heaney

Chapter 25
BRIDEOGS

St Brigid's Strand at Rosadillisk looking north to Cleggan Head and Clare Island in County Mayo, and Brid Coyne, one of many Connemara girls called after the saint.
Picture by Bill Heaney

Here is Miss Brigid dressed in white,
Give her a penny in honour of the night,
Put your hand in your pocket,
Take the weight off your purse,
And this time next year,
May you be none the worse.

In the 1940s the observance of the ***Brideog*** custom was particularly strong in the Connacht counties of Galway and Mayo. Most frequently the custom involved groups of two to ten or more people called Biddy Boys or Biddies carrying an effigy of a baby or a woman from house to house on the eve of the saint's feast day. And it was a much bigger Festival in those days than any other customs concerned with disguise in Ireland, including Hallowe'en. Its purpose was to bring good luck to the homes of spinsters and young single women - and to spur them towards marriage before Lent when the sacrament was banned by the Catholic Church. In some places, including parts of Connemara, a man donned women's clothing and represented the saint and the ceremony included hats of straw, straw ropes on legs, blackened faces and ragged clothing. However, not everyone was disguised and some disapproval was expressed by people who saw the whole exercise as a cash making scam for young boys who were simply repeating the performance of St Stephen's Day wren boys.
Dr Anne O'Dowd in her book ***Straw, Hay & Rushes in Irish Folk Tradition,*** says the group were given eggs or money and pins were stuck in the effigy of a St Brigid's cross or *crois* which they carried. Usually, women would only take part when there were not enough men volunteers to make up the group. In some areas, members of the group, who carried with them

a Brideog, which was a wooden stick or a butter churn wearing a white dress and gaudy ribbons over entwined straw, demanded money for drink in place of the traditional eggs. This didn't make them popular with many people and nor did the fact that they targeted women who they said should get married before Shrove Tuesday.
Also, if these groups were welcomed, and given money for a spree, they would praise and recommend the girls and women they had called on to their male friends – but, if not, they would warn their pals to avoid them. There was also the threat that the curse of Brid, which hung over those who were not generous, would fall upon them. Brigid's girdle, a straw belt with four crosses, was carried by the groups, mainly on the Aran Islands and around Moycullen and others areas of Connemara. The woman of the house was asked to go through the *crois* so that she would be seven times better off a year hence. Details from other places show slight variations in the practice of the custom.
In Aran, Mary, the Mother of God, and St Patrick appeared in the *rann* or verse, recited by the boys who accompanied the *crois*. In Recess, the crois was hung around the doorframe of the house, and all the family, except the father and mother, went out of the house through the crois and walked around the house nine times. The straw girls was a manifestation of the change from winter and darkness to spring and the start of a new agricultural year, with the emphasis on ensuring the well-being of livestock and humans. In the Maam and Rosmuc area, some of the croisanna, or girdles, were made large enough for the cattle to walk through them, ensuring their protection for the next 12 months. In *Fearann an Choirce*, on *Arainn*, the *crois* had only one small cross attached to it and the practice was to go through the *crois*, kiss the cross and ensure that the right foot was the first to step out.

Dressing up and strange practices were part of the Brideog rituals in Letterfrack, Connemara, in the 1940s.

There are seven examples of *crois* in the National Museum of Ireland's Irish Folklife Collection in Castlebar, Co Mayo, of which Anne O'Dowd was Curator for 30 years. All these examples are from Galway. One of them was acquired in 1931 and was given a Tuam provenance and the remaining six were acquired from Connemara in the 1940s where the custom was still observed at that time. So many interesting objects are made of straw and it is sometimes easy to overlook the most common of them and the careful craft that went into making them. Often we see a St Brigid's Cross hanging above a door, a wicker basket topped with turf at the hearth, or the elegance of a thatched roof.

Straw, hay and rushes were utilised throughout the centuries in Ireland for a myriad of such practical uses and rituals, developing an unprecedented store of domestic and agricultural objects abundant in function, folklore and beauty. Anne O'Dowd's exquisitely designed new book celebrates and explores the rich history and tradition of this native craft, featuring almost 400 rare and unpublished images. It is described by the publishers as a 'coffee-table book' but it is much more than that. It will be hard to put down for anyone interested in Irish arts, folklore, history and traditional crafts. It is a richly rewarding read, perhaps even an ideal Christmas present for someone who appreciates all things Irish. The thousand or so objects made from straw, hay and rushes held in the National Museum forms the basis for this beautiful book and its richly informative content. Adorned with hundreds of colour images and drawings, it presents a fascinating insight into Irish crafts and rituals and their ancient origins.

Dr O'Dowd wrote previously *Spalpeens and Tattie Hokers - History and Folklore of the Irish Migratory Worker in Ireland and Britain.* She continues to write on Irish folk life and also works on landscape design projects. Her latest book, published by Irish Academic Press, is available from bookshops and www.iap.ie, at €45.

Author Dr Anne O'Dowd signing a copy of one of her books for Bill Heaney and the cover of Anne's new book, *Straw, Hay & Rushes.*

Chapter 26
CLEGGAN DISASTER

Cleggan Disaster survivor Sheddy Feeney (centre) with friends in Joyce's public house in Cleggan. They are (left to right) Padraig Churchill, Bunny Joyce, Michael MacDonnell, Sheddy Feeney, Johnny Murray, Frank King and Eoin King.
Picture by Bill Heaney

I was born three years after the Cleggan Disaster which happened on the 28th of October, 1927, *recalls Eoin King*. Four boats sailed out from Rosadillisk in Connemara to the fishing ground. It had been raining all days and towards the evening it cleared up. And I can only assume what happened is that the fleet of currachs were in the eye of the hurricane when they went to the fishing ground. Not long after they would have reached the fishing ground and around 7 o'clock in the evening a violent storm blew up. Three of the boats with 16 men were drowned – and one boat came home. Each boat was crewed by five men but on this particular night there were six men in one boat. One boat was owned by my mother's uncle whose name was Martin Murray. He had a crew of five – one would be Patrick Davis, one would be Tommy Lacey, the third was Son of Simon, whose name was Martin Holleran. I cannot be sure what the fifth man's name was. You see we get the names of the different crews mixed up. The other boat was owned by Martin Cloonan and was crewed by himself; his son, Michael, Thomas Delap, Mick Laffey and I believe Michael Feeney and Packey Feeney who

would be cousins, possibly brothers. The other boat was owned by Mark O'Toole with his two brothers, George and Martin, and Mark O'Toole, no relation, and Johnny Murray.
Now the other boat, the boat that returned, was owned by Festy Feeney and that was the only boat that returned from the Cleggan fleet of four. They landed on Sellerna strand. The crew of that boat was Festy Feeney, skipper, Johnny Murray, Sheddy Feeney, a relation of my own but how close I am not sure, Tim Davis, and again I am not sure who the fifth man was. You see, I haven't got all their names. Now it's known from where the boats came ashore and some of the corpses were found that they made a brilliant effort to save themselves. Two of the boats came ashore on top of Cleggan Bay. At that particular time they had no navigation equipment. At that time they sailed by what we called ready reckoning. They estimated the speed at which the boats travelled or drifted and because of the speed they travelled at blown by the force of the hurricane they underestimated the distance they had travelled and for want of a light on Cleggan Pier they got lost at the top of the Bay because they had underestimated their speed. Had there been a light on Cleggan Pier they would have known where to turn to get the shelter of Cleggan Pier. They went out from the strand in Rosadillisk. They anchored on the strand at the village of Rosadillisk. They did not have far to go. But there was no way they could find or land at the place from which they left. They had been drift netting for mackerel in the fishing grounds where they would shoot their nets.
They would be on the fishing grounds half an hour or less before they left. There was no question of them having gone out beyond Bofin. They only went about half a mile from the strand from which they set out. They were drift netting, fishing for mackerel. They drifted with the current. The wind that drove them ashore came from a north westerly direction which blew them on to the shore. The shore was right up the top of Cleggan Bay. There were two boats there and the third one would have been wrecked possibly on the point of Cleggan Head, where the lighthouse now is. The fishing grounds were vast or very expansive. Fishing boats coming out from Bofin would not have any human contact with them because they went the shortest possible distance from their base in Inisbofin to get to their fishing ground – and the number of boats from Bofin – I am not sure but I think there were two boats drowned from Bofin – then again another boat came back to Inisbofin skippered by a man called Matt Concannon.
A total of 25 men were killed altogether. Had there been a light on Cleggan Pier they would know when they could have sought the shelter of the pier but there being no light there they did not know where they were and they were driven ashore and some of them were possibly killed rather than drowned on the shore. They were killed when they were dashed against the rocks some of them – or dashed against the strand. One boat in particular, Johnny Cloonan's boat. Now, there are lots of stories told about this and lots of people will comment on what they did and what they didn't do. Or what they should have done and why other experienced fishermen who should have been out that night did not go out. But who is to know what they done? It had been raining and there was a moderate breeze all day and the wind moved round from a southerly direction to the north, North West. And we can only assume that what actually happened was that they were in the eye of the hurricane when they went fishing and when it blew from the north west that meant they had no knowledge that that was going to happen.
The boat that did survive cut themselves free of their net and ran before the wind. They didn't land where they intended to land. I knew two of the survivors and I have heard the younger man of the two complimented the skipper of the boat saying he had done certain things which

saved them. The skipper told him there was nothing he had done had any bearing on their survival. He did say it was the mercy of God that brought them home. This man who made this comment lost two brothers. He was Sheddy Feeney. His brothers were Mick and Packey. Packey should not have been out that night. He was an extra man on John Cloonan's boat. There were three Lacey brothers, Martin, Mark and George Lacey with whom you had Mark O'Toole and Johnny Murray. Now I can't tell you a whole lot more about it except in regard to the search for bodies. I believe there were six coffins. The next day, or the day after, they were taken into Cleggan and eventually buried in the graveyard in Omey Island.

Marty Coyne, of Rosadillisk, whose Murray relatives were caught up in the Cleggan Disaster. *Picture by Bill Heaney*

There have been certain articles written which are not true. For instance, that there was a ghost boat seen going out to Bofin with the fleet a night or two previous to the disaster. That is not true. That never happened because I know from the survivors of the drowning disaster. They told me themselves it wasn't true. If there were such a boat they would have seen it – but there was no ghost boat. None of the crews of the fishing boats had ever made any comment about that at the time. It only came into the story afterwards. My father fished in this region for a number of years. Having got married, and being a small farmer like they all were, he had given up fishing for the simple reason he had a little bit too much to do at home because of them rearing a family and my mother couldn't content herself with it, particularly when she had been born in Dumbarton and she wasn't reared to being a fisherman's wife. She couldn't content herself like she would have done had she been born locally and brought up with that. He gave up fishing. Lucky for him … if you can say it was lucky. For it brought some hardship afterwards. Anyhow, he wasn't fishing at that time and there were several men who for different reasons were not out fishing that night either. But, call it fate, call it whatever you like, he was not out that night.

Cleggan Bay looking west from Fairy Hill towards the village and Inishbofin.
Picture by Heather Greer

Naturally my mother was heartbroken about what happened, particularly since Martin Murray was her immediate uncle. And he had left a wife and eight children. Now I would say that he would have been one of the saddest cases in that he left the biggest family and possibly the poorest family. George Lacey and Martin Lacey and Tommy Lacey are three brothers who weren't married. Tommy Lacey was fishing with Martin Murray, my mother's cousin. He wasn't married either. Patrick Davis was also a bachelor. Now Johnny Murray was married and had something like five or six of a family. Mark O'Toole was married and left four of a family. Johnny Cloonan, who owned his boat, drowned that night. He left a wife and two sons and two daughters besides. Michael Feeney, Packey Feeney, or Mick Feeney or Mick Laffey, Martin Lacey, George Lacey and Sonny Holleran and Mark Lacey and Tommy Lacey and Patrick Davis were all unmarried. Sixteen of them from Rosadillisk died. The last survivor, Festy Feeney, who was 92 when he died, was buried at Omey in 1992.

There is a love story written by Walter Macken which relates a tale about fishermen meeting a redheaded girl on the road. Any fisherman, to say the least about it, got rather discouraged if he met a woman on the road. It would not necessarily be that she would be a red haired woman, and the women of the place who understood the superstition avoided where possible any reason to be on the road so they would not meet the fishermen going to work. Now there were several taboos, superstitions at that particular time. There were certain animals or birds that were never referred to or their names ever mentioned on the water. You did not take coppers or pennies with you. The fishermen had been known to put them under a stone on the shore and leave them there until they came back. Also they were very reluctant to lend anything to each other while out fishing. If you did lend to someone something he, without your authority, gave you something back. For example they would swap bait for instance, hooks if you were line fishing or perhaps if you did not have any tobacco or rowlocks. If you broke a rowlock and did not have a replacement you would have to get one from another member of the crew. If he gave you one or two or three you gave him three things back.

Every boat at that particular time so far as I know because I have done it myself carried some form of fire. You carried an iron pot or an iron container of some kind that you filled with sand and put hot turf in it, not so much now because you have gas and you have matches and lighters

and that kind of thing. But you carried this pot with the fire in it. They would be out from the fall of night and they would fish until daybreak. The belief was that in the day the fish could see the net whereas at night time they didn't see it.
The fishing ground, was rather confined although the current ran from north east to south west or the opposite way depending on the incoming or outgoing tide. Now being in a landlocked area you could only drift a certain distance before you came on the land so you hauled back your nets and you rowed back up against the current and drifted. If you were lucky you might only make one shot or two. You could hit a shoal of fish which would give you a loaded boat, maybe two or three thousand fish, not so much in a currach because there were very few currachs fishing at the time. But you see at that time fish were sold by count – rather than by numbers or by weight. The count was known as the long hundred. It consisted of six score and six fishes which was 126 rather than 100 single fish. Now prices were not great at the time and you – it could be anything from – let's compare it with today's price, it would be half a crown to £1 a hundred fish depending on the scarcity of the fish and what the market was like. Now when you took quite a good catch which could be anything from 1,000 to 2,000 fish you rowed home. You would get this on one night. You brought them into Cleggan and they were often caught up twisted in your net and you had to untangle those fish by hand. You tied up and you put your nets out on the pier and you waited for morning for the fish buyers to come and there might be an auction or it might be that you had some buyer that you were closer to than others and you might get a market. Others might not get a market.
If they got too much fish to export or to send to the markets fresh from Cleggan then they would salt them. They set up a system on Cleggan Pier where the fish were stretched and washed and salted and stored in barrels. And sold later through the company. Cured mackerel. Sometimes you often found that you got herring instead of mackerel because sometimes you were in the happy position where your nets caught both herring and mackerel unless it were too late in the ear when the herring had spawned and got too thin and they could go through the nets. Then you might only catch a very small quantity. The fish were carted into Clifden and from there to Galway. You had fish buyers of whose names I am aware of. You had Deasy and Nolan and Hanlon. I think those three fish merchants were based in Galway, where most of our catch was sold.
Emotionally the impact of the Cleggan Disaster was desperate – it was unbelievable how it affected people. It manifested itself in the grief of the people, how they cried and mourned for those people. And, I mean it was only natural that the people who lost their breadwinners – there had to be a financial impact. Fishing was the most important money earner of all at that time. They all had little bits of land whereon they kept a cow or two from which they got milk and butter for part of the year …
But mothers still sent their children to sleep at night with hope and a song in their heart, this beautiful lullaby:

Connemara Cradle Song

On the wings of the wind o'er the deep rolling sea
Angels are coming to watch o'er thy sleep
Angels are coming to watch over thee
So list to the wind coming over the sea

Chorus:

Hear the wind blow, love, hear the wind blow
Lean your head over and hear the wind blow

Oh, winds of the night, may your fury be crossed,
May no one who's dear to our island be lost
Blow the winds gently, calm be the foam
Shine the light brightly and guide them back home

Chorus

The currachs are sailing way out on the blue
Laden with herring of silvery hue
Silver the herring and silver the sea
And soon there'll be silver for baby and me

Chorus

The currachs tomorrow will stand on the shore
And daddy goes sailing, no never no more
The nets will be drying, the oars put away
And daddy is home babe and home he will stay.

Memorials to the victims of the Cleggan Disaster in Inishbofin (left) and Cleggan village, near the pier. *Pictures by Peter Walsh and Rodger Scullion*

Chapter 27
EMIGRATION

Connemara ponies shelter from the rain at a deserted cottage near Claddaghduff.
Picture by Bill Heaney

Emigration has been a problem in the West of Ireland and particularly in this area of Connemara for nearly two centuries. Immediately after the Cleggan Disaster there was a Disaster Fund set up. It was very well subscribed to, but it was very badly handled. I would not have a clue about how much money came into it but I do know that the wrong man was put in charge of it. He was Monsignor McAlpine, parish priest of Clifden, *Eoin King recalls.* It was not the local priest at Claddaghduff, although he would have been consulted. He played a key role in raising funds. Sure even Guinness's plane, Arthur Guinness of the brewery's private plane, came over Cleggan Bay at the time, searching for corpses. Sixteen people were drowned from Cleggan. I am not familiar with the exact numbers lost from Bofin. There were three boats drowned and each boat had a crew of five. But John and Martin Cloonan's boat had a crew of six that particular night. Packey Feeney just went along for the ride. He was Sheddy's brother. Sheddy would only be 17 when that happened.

There were an awful lot of families in the village at that time. To give you an idea in so far as I can recall, there were two or three Holloran families, an O'Toole family, a Lacey family, a Cloonan family, four Lacey families in fact. The amount of money that was collected for the families of the victims was handled by the parish priest. I have no idea how much, but I do know a certain amount of time elapsed between the collecting of the funds and the organising of what was paid to the families. But what I do know is that there is no trace whatsoever of the

amount of money that would have accumulated in interest while the money was in the bank. It was not so much in dispute because 90 per cent of people were not that financially well up that they could work it out But in later years when people were able to work it out, that since the money had been in the bank for such a long time it must have made interest – and quite an amount of interest.
The coffins, as the remains were found, were kept in a store in Cleggan. There were six coffins in that particular store house at that particular time with the remains of six people in them, six of the victims. They were taken in procession to Our Lady Star of the Sea church in Claddaghduff. They were buried in Omey Island and over the grave an impressive Celtic cross was erected. The people here searched continuously for the remains of the other victims. In actual fact some of them were never found, so you can safely say that the search is going on yet.

The windswept graveyard on Omey Island where the victims of the Cleggan Disaster are buried. *Picture by Bill Heaney*

I suppose the funds which were collected and given to those people helped to a certain extent. I don't believe any house went down as a result of that, except possibly two. One Lacey family, George, Martin and Mark, their house would have closed down after their mother died and Sonny Holleran also, who I think was unmarried. His house would have closed down after he died. The rest of them – you cannot say it had any lasting effect on life. As the families grew up, some of them emigrated and those who did not emigrate went back to the sea again in another way, lobster fishing. The disaster that took place did not necessarily mean they did not fish again the next year. There is fishing and there is the sea and there will be fishing disasters but you cannot let these things destroy your livelihood. I would say that the women's attitude was that they would rather that their families would emigrate than go back to sea again. They encouraged them to emigrate and a lot of them would have emigrant relatives anyhow who would make a special effort to bring them to the States rather than to leave them there to possibly suffer the same fate as their fathers and uncles had suffered. The Cleggan Disaster Fund did not do a great deal. The only thing it did in that particular instance was to give employment. There was a special grant given to build a road from the road outside the house here at Emlough – Cathie O'Sullivan's cottage - down as far as Mick Lacey's place at Rosadillisk. That road was built there after that. That was all the State aid they ever got and they did not put any money in people's pockets. It did not buy them land, it did not buy them cattle, and it did not resettle them.

Sheddy Feeney (left) and Eoin King, both of whose remains are interred in the graveyard in Omey.

Today Sheddy Feeney's tombstone is an open book. And one side of the book is in loving memory of Sheddy Feeney, last survivor of the Cleggan Drowning Disaster, RIP. Erected by the De Courcey family. And on the other page of it there is: *It's not the host that rules the house but the love that reigns therein.* It's quite nice that mind you, a favourite saying of Sheddy's. There are just two people living in Rosadillisk now who are the relatives of any of the people who were victims of the disaster. They are Marty Coyne, grandson of Martin Murray, and Feichin O'Toole, grandson of Mark O'Toole. There are no others – no connection – despite the fact that there are three other families living in Emlough. There was a time when you had a fishing fleet that went out from Aughrusbeg and Emlough and Rosadillisk that fished across the whole of Cleggan Bay. But they wore out.

The Cleggan Disaster wasn't the only thing that happened to discourage them. There have been drownings, other drownings, in Cleggan Bay over the years. One of these was a family boat; Cottingham was their name, from Aughrusbeg. There was never a resolution to concentrate more on the land than on the sea. I was inclined towards the sea but you see at that particular time just after the Second World War the market failed. During the war there was a market for anything you could catch that fed into the food chain, but after the War things began to improve. The fishing went down because you didn't have a market. There was a kind of a slump and the next best market was for lobster.

The biggest farm around here would be ten to 12 acres. My own place was 16 acres – but that was because it was two farms together, those of both sets of my grandparents. My uncle Michael emigrated in 1921. The size of the house was about 35ft by 14ft. You had no income at all apart from what you got from your produce and the couple of cattle that you could raise and sell and mostly that went to pay for the rent, the rent of the land. We didn't acquire rightful ownership to our land until about 1932 or 1935. That was from the landlords up until then. We never owned it then. It was extortionate rent. For instance for my uncle emigrated in 1920 or 1921 and that was when the nobby fishing genuinely failed in Cleggan. He was fishing up until then. Sir Richard Burridge was the landowner. He owned land all the way into Gort into East Galway. There were Ayres and Hanleys; those were the three landlords in the area. They probably owned hundreds of thousands of acres, but they put in agents. What they did was let portions of the land to agents for a certain price. Those agents in turn sub-let it to the poorer tenants and bled them for what they could get from them. It wasn't a question of setting the land to you for face value; it was a question of setting the land to you for what they could get out of you. Rack rent. You had the tithes when you had to pay a certain amount of money to the Church of Ireland to finance a religion in which you didn't partake and in which you did not believe. Upwards to 1932 my father was expected to raise £28 a year to pay the rent on what was in the region of 14 acres of land. That was £2 an acre. The product of an acre of land at that particular time, there is no way if you look at it this way, if you planted an acre of potatoes which returned you five tonnes that you sold for three pence a stone which was two shillings or 10 pence a cwt in today's money. So there was no way you could produce enough to pay the rent anyhow, but they didn't give a damn whether you could or not. You had to find it or you would be out in the cold. Now, some people ... had nothing.

An abandoned cabin at Claddaghduff looking out towards High Island.
Picture by Bill Heaney

Chapter 28
SMOKE'S UP AT SHEDDY'S

Thomas Coohill from Cleggan cutting turf. *Picture by Heather Greer*

One of my favourite poems is about turf cutting. It was written by my namesake, famous Seamus Heaney, the Nobel laureate. In the poem, Seamus describes the sound of a slane, a spade for slicing through turf, and the rasping sound it makes as it sinks into gravelly ground. The late and greatly lamented Seamus, who told me of his visits to Cleggan and Inishbofin when I met him in Edinburgh, recalled watching his father, Patrick, digging on the bog. I told him that I too had my day on the bog. It was about 50 years ago I was asked by Mary King if I would go out from Aughrusbeg to 'the mountain' with something to eat for Eoin. The 'mountain' wasn't a mountain at all, of course. It was the Lachtanabba Bog on the road from Cleggan to Clifden. And it was hardly an undulation or even a hill, never mind a mountain. It was a long walk from the back of beyond though, past Cleggan Pier, through the village Main Street – the one and only street - and up to the bog, where Eoin was digging, digging, as it says in the Heaney poem. I brought him tea in a bottle. The neck was stuffed with old newspaper. This was to stop the tea slopping inside the makeshift bag Mary had given me to carry Eoin's 'pieces'. Or wetting the old woollen sock in which she had placed the bottle to

keep the tea warm. Pieces are what we call a workman's sandwiches in Scotland. Mary had admirably not abandoned that vernacular on her odyssey from Clydeside to Connemara, and the bleach fields of the Vale of Leven, where she once worked.
Eoin King was ready for his dinner, which is what the Connemara people call lunch and is eaten in the middle of the day. I think it was slices of bright yellow cheese and soda bread, baked by Mary herself in an iron pot on the turf fire in her wee thatched cottage. This was a fire that was never allowed to go out. It remained lit from the day a family moved into a house until the day they left it. And even then they carried the red hot cinders to their new abode to make a fire there. If they were emigrating, they would carry it to a neighbour's house and ask them to mind it for them. The turf fire was used for everything from boiling potatoes to feeding the hens – and humans - to making bread, cooking and hanging down the kettle to boil water for tea. Ireland was fortunate to have its turf bogs, particularly during the Second World War when there was a coal shortage. It was the only form of energy in Connemara, where there was no running water, and light was provided by paraffin lamps until electricity was introduced in the late 'Fifties.

Ireland's most famous postcard produced by John Hinde and Company is this photograph of two children taken with their donkey on a Connemara bog. And the interior of a traditional farmhouse at the Dan O'Hara homestead, near Clifden.

The fire was the focal point of the house, of course. The mantelpiece was adorned with a crucifix, statues of the Blessed Virgin and the Infant of Prague and a pair of wally dugs, which you can see in the photograph reproduced above. If only we could remember all the news, good and bad, happy and sad, that was broken there and those many stories that were told around the old turf fire, while the flames were roaring up the chimney. The blue smoke and sweet smell, some might call it perfume, from the turf fire is memorable. It's not only from the heather that the wind gathers perfume as it blows. Turf smoke is a favourite smell, a delightful odour that fills the nostrils with pleasure and tells you that you are home. That smoke served many purposes, not least of which was what its presence spiralling into the air of a cold, frosty morning signalled. It helps people keep a watchful eye on their elderly neighbours. I remember one morning Eoin King going out to 'the street' for a look at the weather and coming back with the news that 'Smoke's up at Sheddy's,' which meant the old man was well and up and about down the road at Rosadillisk.

There was obviously a technique to digging on the bog. Eoin was good at everything from planting and sowing and looking after cattle – even building his own new house – and he was naturally very good at harvesting turf. I gave him a hand with the stooks and stacked the sods in a way that allowed the wind to blow through them and dry them off. Only then would they be suitable to use as fuel for the fire. Eoin took great pride in his work, much of which he tackled at pace, but he slowed down when it came to turf cutting. Like Heaney's old man, Eoin King could handle a slane. He cut into the chocolate brown bog with measured strokes. The poet said his grandfather cut more turf in a day than any other man on the bog. I never yet met the man who cut more turf than Eoin at Lachtanabba Bog. He was a perfectionist 'nicking and slicing, heaving heavy sods over his shoulder, going down for the good turf. Digging.'
Cutting turf in bad weather can be a penance, but the day I did it with Eoin, the sun was shining, corncrakes and cuckoos were competing with each other for attention and a lark was hovering high overhead. The outlook out over Cleggan Bay and Inishbofin was astoundingly beautiful, worthy of a painting by Paul Henry himself. I remember stretching out and going to sleep. I resembled a Red Indian when I woke up. The camomile lotion was called for to treat the sunburn that night. The straw mattress did its worst on my back, which I had so stupidly over exposed to the sun.

All the implements one needs for the makings of a good dinner and a roaring turf fire on display at the National Folk Museum in Castlebar, Co Mayo, and some lads in Clifden bringing home the turf. *Picture by Bill Heaney*

One of the highlights of the Connemara year is bringing home the turf, which is a different from digging it. I took part in it once when we had a *meithal*, which is when neighbours gather together to help one another with the hard work attached to living on a small farm. PJ De Courcey volunteered his tractor and trailer, which meant we didn't have to resort to borrowing from Festy and Mick Lacey donkeys and panniers, like the ones used by the children in the famous John Hinde postcard. I don't know how many trailer loads we brought back from the bog, but there were quite a few and everyone mucked in. It is a tradition that the workers are fed and watered by the people they are helping. Mary King laid on a spread fit for a prince and we ate heartily and sunk gallons of tea and, would you believe it, some bottles of stout. It was a great day altogether.

Turf, of course, was used by fishermen for laying down a fire for cooking on currachs and Galway hookers, the workboats of the West of Ireland seaboard. Every one of these boats carried some form of fire. There was an iron pot or an iron container of some kind that the fishermen and boatmen filled with sand and put hot turf in it in so they could cook when they were on the water for hours on end. It was also used to heat the classrooms of country schools and children took a few sods with them from home to keep the fire going throughout the school year. If you want to see bread being baked on a turf fire then you need travel no further than Clifden to the Dan O'Hara Homestead. The award winning Heritage Centre and Farmhouse includes bed and breakfast accommodation and is just 6km from Clifden on the N59 in Connemara. Overlooked by the majestic Twelve Bens mountain range, this agri-tourism enterprise is run by Martin and Nora and their family on a traditional Irish hill farm. It's now almost 25 years since they diversified into agri-tourism and decided to share with visitors the history, heritage, culture and traditions of stunningly beautiful Connemara. The farm has cattle, sheep and the world famous Connemara ponies with a few friendly donkeys in the fields and lively chickens strutting their stuff in the yard. The centre is based around the restored pre-Famine cottage of Dan O' Hara, who was forced to emigrate in the 1840s when he was evicted from his home. Guided tours are both entertaining and educational and offer demonstrations of traditional farming activities such as turf cutting, sheep herding, soda bread making on an open fire and games for the children. Tours are suitable for student groups, school tours, active retired people and corporate or incentive groups. There are interesting audio visual aids and the artefacts room has articles and items on display of *Connemara through the Ages.* Other items of interest at the Centre include reconstructions of a crannog and an ancient ring fort. There's a comfortable restaurant where you can enjoy morning coffee or afternoon tea or lunch if that suits you. And there is a craft shop with souvenirs and traditional Irish gifts, not to mention internet access and free parking for coach parties. Admission charges are modest and special group rates available for guided tours. You can contact Paula or Nora info@connemaraheritage.com or telephone 003539521246.

Baking soda bread on a turf fire at the Dan O'Hara Homestead in Clifden and a tractor driver with turf aboard stops to see a Gaelic football match.

Meanwhile, Bord na Móna, the Turf Board, have announced that the industrial scale exploitation of Ireland's bogs will end by 2030. The really large bogs are in places like Prosperous in the Bog of Allen, where I once watched my boys play Gaelic football in the shadow of two huge turf-fed power station chimneys. The company plans to transform itself into an alternative energy company, centred on biomass, wind and solar power. Peat briquettes, a popular winter fuel in many homes, even nowadays in Connemara, will be replaced by biomass briquettes. Thankfully though 'private' bogs, such as those utilised by people like Thomas Coohill of Cleggan, will continue to exist. Describing its plans as 'the biggest change of use involving Irish land in modern history', the semi-State company will open a new wind farm every year for the next seven years, according to its new chief executive, Mike Quinn. Co-located with many such farms will be solar energy farms. None are planned for Connemara, where stern opposition to wind farms would be a given. Wind Aware Ireland, which opposes wind farms, welcomed an end to peat harvesting and reinstatement of bogs, and new emphasis on biomass. 'However, the continued development of wind energy cannot be considered sustainable, economically, environmentally or socially,' it said in a statement. Friends of the Earth said continuing to burn peat for power until 2030 was a 'decade too late', adding that 'public money would be much better invested in kick-starting a rooftop solar revolution'. Peaceful Connemara would be a most unlikely place for a revolution to start, and certainly not a solar revolution. The rain comes around too often, although snow is only an occasional visitor. But putting up with a soft day and the rain on the wind, work like bringing home the turf or laying down a few sods on the fire, is no hardship:

May the blessing of the rain be on you—
the soft sweet rain.
May it fall upon your spirit
so that all the little flowers may spring up
and shed their sweetness on the air
May the blessing of the great rains be on you
may they beat upon your spirit
and wash it fair and clean,
and leave there many a shining pool
where the blue of heaven shines
and sometimes a star

Anon

A slane, which is a spade for cutting turf, and Bill Heaney with Festy Lacey's donkey.